The Struggle for the Health and Legal Protection of Farm Workers
El Cortito

The Struggle for the Health and Legal Protection of Farm Workers
El Cortito

MAURICE "MO" JOURDANE

FOREWORD BY HENRY A. J. RAMOS
INTRODUCTION BY MARC GROSSMAN

Arte Público Press
Houston, Texas

This volume is made possible through grants from the James Irvine Foundation, the California Wellness Foundation, the National Endowment for the Arts (a federal agency), the Charles Stewart Mott Foundation, and the City of Houston through The Cultural Arts Council of Houston, Harris County.

Recovering the past, creating the future

Arte Público Press
University of Houston
452 Cullen Performance Hall
Houston, Texas 77204-2004

Cover design by James Brisson.
Cover photo courtesy of Sam Vestel.

Jourdane, Maurice.
    The Struggle for the Health and Legal Protection of Farm Workers: El Cortito / Maurice Jourdane; foreword by Henry A. Ramos, introduction by Marc Grossman.
        p.   cm. — (Hispanic civil rights series)
    ISBN 1-55885-423-1 (pbk. : alk. hardcover)
    ISBN 1-55885-426-6 (cloth : alk. hardcover)
        1. Agricultural implements—Law and legislation—California.
    2. Hoes—Health aspects—California—Central Valley. 3. Mexican American agricultural laborers—Health and hygiene—California—Central Valley. 4. Mexican American agricultural laborers—Civil rights—California—Central Valley.   I. Title.   II. Series.
    KFC589.A4J68 2004
    331.6′27207945—dc22   2004041079
                                                                                     CIP

∞ The paper used in this publication meets the requirements of the American National Standard for Information Sciences—Permanence of Paper for Printed Library Materials, ANSI Z39.48-1984.

4 5 6 7 8 9 0 1 2 3   10 9 8 7 6 5 4 3 2 1

To farm workers who stoop in the fields from dawn to dusk to put food on our tables and to those who have struggled to provide farm workers the respect they deserve.

Contents

Acknowledgments ix

Foreword by Henry A. J. Ramos xi

Author's Note xvi

Introduction by Marc Grossman xvii

The Struggle for Health and Legal Protection of Farm
    Workers: *El Cortito* 1

Acknowledgments

I wish to acknowledge Gustavo López and Sebastián Carmona, whose sacrifices led me to the fields, and to the hundreds of thousands farm workers who led me to the *cortito* case. I would like to thank Dennis Renault, photographer Bill Daniels, and the Vestal family who gave me permission to use their political cartoons and timeless photographs; Marc Grossman who donated his work on the John Steinbeck/César Chávez connection; Leti Bocanegra of the Steinbeck Center whose help and urging led to the completion of this book; Mirandi Babitz, Luis López, Marie Arvette, and Carlos Bowker for reading the manuscript in its first stages and for encouraging me to tell the story; Eric Brazil, former city editor of the Salinas *Californian*, David Steingass, and Terry McDonnell for making valuable suggestions on how to tell the story; and Nicolás Kanellos, Ph.D. and the staff at Arte Público Press who transformed a rough draft by an unknown *güero* into a book.

I want to acknowledge Jerry Cohen, Marty Glick, Ralph Abascal, Denny Powell, Dave Kirkpatrick, Luis Jaramillo, and Susan Alva, the attorneys who have dedicated their lives to the farm worker and immigrant struggle.

I thank César Chávez, Dolores Huerta, Ladislao Pineda, Héctor De la Rosa, and Adelina Gurrola who encouraged me to stick with the farm workers' effort.

Finally, I wish to thank and acknowledge my wife Olivia Flores who was always by my side with words of encouragement; my children Jackie and Jonathan who, from their birth, patiently listened to the stories that underlie this book; and my mother who taught me that the color of one's skin, the language one speaks, and whether one is rich or poor, is irrelevant to their inherent goodness, their values, or their birthright to equality.

Foreword

The struggle of Hispanic farm workers for rights and justice in California and other states across the Southwest is one of the most compelling stories of recent U.S. social and legal advancement. This struggle, led by the late United Farm Workers (UFW) union founder, César E. Chávez, was an informing chapter of the nation's civil rights gains of the 1960s and 1970s. During these years, American political leaders no less significant than Robert F. Kennedy, Martin Luther King, Jr., and Edmund G. (Jerry) Brown, Jr. were drawn to become fundamental champions of the farm workers' cause.

Maurice ("Mo") Jourdane was a young staff attorney of the California Rural Legal Assistance (CRLA) organization that helped to protect farm worker rights through federally supported legal interventions during the UFW's incipiency. His work at CRLA helped to secure several of the farm workers' most significant victories in their campaign for justice. Jourdane, for example, played a key role in challenging the now prohibited California practice of placing Hispanic children—and especially farm worker children—in classes designed for the mentally retarded owing to low test scores resulting from standardized aptitude testing in English, rather than Spanish. His efforts also helped to secure the employment and free speech rights of teachers and students who supported progressive causes, such as the farm worker and anti-Vietnam War struggles, as well as the right of union representatives to organize in the fields and company housing complexes where agricultural laborers worked and lived in California's Central Valley.

But Jourdane's greatest contribution to the farm workers' advancement was his relentless—and ultimately successful—effort to end California agricultural employers' required use of the short-handled hoe by laborers in the state's lucrative lettuce, celery, sugar beet, and strawberry industries. The short hoe, known by Hispanic farm workers in Spanish as *el cortito* (the short one), was the cause of severe and permanent crippling among these laborers. It required workers to spend as many as ten to twelve hours each day (often in more than 90 degree heat) stooped over in literally backbreaking posture to complete their tasks of thinning, weeding, and harvesting the land on behalf of agribusiness employers who profited immensely both from the workers' exceedingly low-cost labor, as well as their docility. Lacking union representation and affordable legal assistance, these Mexican workers (and their predecessors from China, Japan, the Philippines, and other nations) were perennially subjected to slave-like employment conditions and nearly uninhabitable company housing for nearly a century prior to the commencement of the UFW's and CRLA's work.

Jourdane, the product ironically of a small farm-owning family from conservative Orange County, became the unlikely catalyst for change related to San Diego's short-hoe practice. For nearly a decade, he relentlessly researched and advocated for a state ban of the short hoe. In direct negotiations with employers, in administrative hearings, and in the courts, Jourdane faced formidable early resistance to his efforts from growers, and strong political opposition from the conservative, pro-grower administration of then California Governor (and later U.S. President) Ronald Reagan. But in the mid-1970s, with the election of liberal former California Governor Jerry Brown, Jourdane and the CRLA were able to make significant strides toward improving farm labor conditions and rights in the state. Ultimately, by working effectively with farm labor leaders via the UFW (including its founder César E. Chávez), other CRLA attorneys and volunteers, and a plethora of medical experts and aggrieved workers, Jourdane was able to convince the California Supreme Court to compel the state Industrial Relations Board to mandate the short hoe's discontinued use by growers and their workers in the fields. His victory on behalf of the workers was a critical advance in the farm labor struggle and helped to lead the way to Governor Brown's establishment of a wholly new and far more equitable regulatory protocol governing California agricultural employees.[1]

Jourdane's recount of his efforts to assist the farm workers offers a startling reminder of just how much de jure and de facto injustice prevailed in California and other western states as recently as the late 1970s, where Hispanic agricultural laborers and immigrants were concerned. Reading his recollections today, moreover, one is reminded of continuing similar injustices that inform contemporary Latino (and other immigrant/minority) labor struggles in the garment, service, and heavy production industries of the nation. Jourdane's historical summation of the farm workers' struggle for justice thus reminds us that, despite real gains that were achieved by and for California farm laborers in the 1960s and 1970s, still today much remains to be done to protect worker health and civil rights.

Books like this one thus play a critical role in raising public consciousness and encouraging needed reforms, both from an historical and a contemporary perspective. Younger readers—both Hispanic and non-Hispanic—who did not directly experience the harsh realities of the times that necessitated the efforts of early public interest lawyers like Jourdane, should especially benefit from exposure to his story. By reading Jourdane, they may take into account the merits of considering the ways in which they might play a constructive role in addressing continuing social and economic injustice by pursuing an activist path in law, education, or community and labor organizing. They may furthermore gain insight into how much commitment, patience, and hard work is often required to forge even the most basic advancements in civil and human rights. Finally, they may gain a deeper appreciation of their own privileges and opportunities in contemporary society and a stronger sense of social responsibility to play a part in positively shaping the social justice history still to be made in their own lifetimes.

These are the primary aims of the University of Houston Arte Público Press (APP) Hispanic Civil Rights Series that makes this pub-

---

[1]Brown's policy established the California Agricultural Labor Relations Board to ensure fairer and more equitable farm labor practices and grievance procedures in the state.

lication possible: to educate, to inform, and to inspire Americans of all backgrounds—and especially younger Americans—relative to the Hispanic community's historical and ongoing struggle for justice in the United States. With support from the Charles Stewart Mott Foundation, the Rockefeller Foundation, the California Wellness Foundation, the James Irvine Foundation, and the Ewing Marion Kauffman Foundation, the Civil Rights Series is producing more than twenty original works by and about many of the leading protagonists of the post-World War II civil rights victories of Latinos.

Raising awareness about these many contributions to U.S. social advancement and quality of life is more important than ever, as Hispanics emerge to become the nation's new minority of record. With now more than 35 million individuals comprising the national Hispanic community, and a burgeoning youth population that demographers predict will result in fully one in four Americans being of Latino heritage by the year 2050, it is imperative for all citizens and longtime residents of the United States to gain a more evolved comprehension of Hispanic people, and for Hispanic Americans themselves (along with their closest friends and allies) to tell the stories of their experiences and social justice victories over recent decades.

By lifting up these affirmative stories and the voices of leaders who helped to shape them, Arte Público Press seeks to develop the texture of recorded U.S. history in ways that elevate public recognition of the Hispanic role in defining what it means to be an American. It also hopes to encourage expanded public dialogue about the important continuing social justice work that still needs to be attended in Latino and other communities of the United States that confront enduring inequities.

Mo Jourdane's book, *The Struggle for the Health and Legal Protection of Farm Workers:* El Cortito, is a truly important addition to our Series. We are especially grateful to Luz Vega Marquis of the Marguerite Casey Foundation, whose trustee contribution as a board member of the California Wellness Foundation helped to supplement our financial support to make this publication possible. An immigrant herself to California during the 1960s and a longtime advocate of expanded philanthropic and other institutional investment in the rights and opportunities of historically disadvantaged groups, Luz's support of our work provides a shining example of the community leadership and social responsibility that we seek to encourage through the APP Civil Rights Series. We are deeply indebted to her and others who have made essential grants to assist this work.

Henry A. J. Ramos
Executive Editor
Hispanic Civil Rights Series
Arte Público Press

Author's Note

To the best of my recollection after obtaining confirmation from the farm workers, attorneys who represented the farm workers, and the community workers with whom I worked, this story tells of events that occurred in California fields during the 1960s and 1970s. Some names have been changed to protect our clients' right to privacy and to preserve the attorney-client privilege. The words used in conversations that took place years ago are those I recall. While I am sure the words I use are not precise, they reflect my recollection of the substance and tenor of the conversations. The events presented all occurred. The views expressed herein are my views as an attorney who represented farm workers in the Salinas Valley from 1968 through 1980. One of America's finest historians, Howard Zinn, said it best: "There is no such thing as a pure fact, innocent of interpretation. Behind every fact presented to the world—by a teacher, a writer, anyone—is a judgment. The judgment that has been made is that this fact is important, and that other facts, omitted, are not important."[1] I have tried to present the facts to the best of the recollection of the participants I have been able to locate.

---

[1] Howard Zinn. *A People's History of the United States* (New York: Harper & Row, 1980).

Introduction

John Steinbeck's *The Grapes of Wrath* is more than a classic novel exposing a dark underside of the California dream. It raised widespread public awareness about the plight of migrant farm workers and set the stage for the rise decades later of César Chávez's movement.

Just as literature and history are sometimes linked, so are John Steinbeck and César Chávez. Communities across California are honoring Steinbeck with events encouraging people to read his various works, which many view as one of America's greatest bodies of literature. So this is a good time to recount those links.

Steinbeck carefully based the characters and subjects of his three novels chronicling farm labor strife—*The Grapes of Wrath*, *In Dubious Battle,* and *Of Mice and Men*—on real people and events. Much of the material for those early books came from the time he spent around his birthplace on the Central Coast and in the Central Valley.

The government-run farm labor camp that offered the Joad family the only respite during its troubled journey in *The Grapes of Wrath* was based on the Sunset Camp, between Arvin and Lamont, south of Bakersfield. Fred Ross, the man who actually ran that camp shortly after Steinbeck left the area, was a little known but remarkable community organizer whose career spanned seven decades.

Around the time Ross was managing the Sunset Camp, an eleven-year old boy began following the migrant trails of California with his destitute family. As with many of the Depression-era Okies from *The Grapes of Wrath*, the banks took César Chávez's parents' small family farm in the Gila River Valley near Yuma, Arizona.

Like the Joads, the Chávezes worked the fields and vineyards of the southern San Joaquin Valley during that time. But Chávez and Ross didn't meet until later. Segregation was the practice, if not the rule, and the Sunset Camp was for Anglos.

The two met for the first time a decade and a half later, in 1952. Ross was organizing the Saul Alinsky-affiliated Community Service Organization, then the most militant and effective civic action, civil rights group among Latinos in California. In the late spring of that year, Ross came to the eastside San Jose barrio of Sal Si Puedes (get out if you can) and sought out Chávez, who was laboring in nearby apricot orchards.

That encounter "led to a lot of things," Chávez said much later. Chávez credited Ross with discovering and training him, and—over forty years—becoming his best friend.

Another link to Steinbeck came out of the blue in the summer of 1971, one year after Central Valley table-grape growers signed their first contracts with Chávez's United Farm Workers, capping five years of strikes and boycotts. Chávez was in his office at "Forty Acres," then the UFW's headquarters just outside Delano. I was a young Chávez aide working on a summer project during a break from college.

His secretary informed Chávez that "an old guy" was in the lobby asking to speak to someone about times past. "I'm busy, have him talk to one of the organizers," Chávez replied. About three hours later she said the old man hadn't left.

"What's his name?" Chávez asked.

"Pat Chambers," the secretary said.

Chávez's face lit up, he bolted down the hall, and Chambers, Chávez, his driver, and I spent the rest of the afternoon driving around Delano and talking. Mostly, I listened.

Chambers was a lead organizer with the Communist-led Cannery and Agricultural Workers' Industrial Union (CAWIU). He led the biggest field walkouts of the early and mid-1930s, including the Corcoran cotton strike of 1933.

Before Chávez, most farm union leaders were nonfarm workers, outsiders sometimes aloof from the people they tried to organize. Not Chambers. He lived among the workers of all races who fed, housed, and protected him. Carey McWilliams, in his classic 1939 exposé

Factories in the Fields, noted that Chambers was "a small, quiet, soft-spoken man, but a person of great courage and significance"—a description not unlike that offered years later about Chávez.[1]

One of Chamber's bodyguards in the '30s was Gonzalo Flores, Chávez's cousin by marriage. When Chávez was young, he listened raptly to tales of this legendary farm labor organizer, Pat Chambers. Chambers was convicted in 1934 for violating California's criminal syndicalism law. It banned "advocating, teaching or aiding and abetting . . . unlawful methods of terrorism as a means of accomplishing a change in industrial ownership or control"—which in Chambers' case included union organizing. He was released after serving time in San Quentin, but never returned to organizing, instead becoming a union carpenter in San Pedro.

Chambers avoided coming to Delano during the five-year grape strike, he added, out of fear Chávez would be red-baited because of CAWIU's Communist ties. But on that bright summer day, Chávez took Chambers to visit his cousin, Gonzalo Flores, who by then was elderly and disabled by diabetes. The two men remembered each other warmly and reminisced.

A few weeks later, Chambers returned to Delano. Chávez was gone, so I met with him. Since Chambers and Steinbeck were in the same region at the same time, I asked Chambers if they ever met. Chambers responded with a cascade of swear words. I quickly dropped the subject.

Later, Ross said some believed Chambers had provided material that Steinbeck used to characterize the communist labor organizer in *In Dubious Battle,* which depicts a strike that turns violent—a theory I later heard confirmed by Steinbeck scholars. Perhaps if someone wrote a book like that about me, I wouldn't like him either.

Marc Grossman
Longtime aide to César Chávez

---

[1]Carey McWilliams, *Factories in the Field: The Story of Migratory Farm Labor in California* (Boston: Little, Brown, and Company, 1939).

One

DURING THE LATE 1960s through the mid-1970s, I began my career in law as a representative of California Rural Legal Assistance (CRLA), one of the early federally supported entities of the War on Poverty, dedicated to providing free legal services to the poor. Our focus was primarily on low-income farm workers and their family members, who were frequently victims of abusive employers and labor contractors in the California Central Valley.

One early morning during the course of my tenure at CRLA, I found myself doing practical research in the fields for a potential case. The issue involved the use of the short hoe, known by Mexican farm laborers as *el cortito* (the short one). Little did I know at the time that this work would dramatically change my life, and, more importantly, the lives of farm laborers across the state of California.

The brisk night wind rushed down the Salinas Valley. I zipped up my windbreaker as I crossed the rural road. Héctor stood with a forty-ish-looking farm worker in the reddish glow of the Tecate Cerveza sign near the *cantina* door. "Jourdane," Héctor said, "this is my *compadre* Sebastián Carmona."

A couple hours later, the *cantina* was loud and smoky. Sliding the pool cue between my arched index finger and thumb, taking aim at the orange five ball, I asked the salt-and-pepper-haired Carmona if he knew what caused his back injury.

"I think I am just getting too old to bend over all day in the field," he replied in Spanish.

Failing to sink the orange ball, I walked to the small round table and picked up the can of Tecate. "What do you do?" I asked Carmona in Spanish. "I know you're a farm worker, but what do you do specifically?"

"Thin and weed plants with the *cortito*."

"What's the *cortito*?"

"A hoe with a very short handle. *Cortito* is how we say short one in Spanish. I have one in the car. I'll show you."

Moments later, in his faded Levi's but neatly pressed white shirt, Carmona returned with a hoe having a normal-sized metal blade and an eight-inch-long wooden handle.

"Because of this short handle," he explained, handing me the hoe, "we must bend over to the ground to do our work."

I had seen the *cortito* before, once on my grandparents' farm when I was a child and another time displayed on a shelf in the office of an attorney with whom I worked, Marty Glick. One of Glick's dreams was to someday get the tool banned.

My pulse raced. "Does your back hurt just when you work or all the time?" I asked.

"All the time, but especially when I bend over."

While we talked, each of us getting up from the table to shoot, friends of Carmona joined us. Carmona told them he was telling the lawyer about the *cortito*.

"I am Efraín Camacho," the eldest-appearing said in Spanish, extending a callused brown hand. "Like Sebastián, I worked with the *cortito* for many years. I am only forty-four, but I can no longer work because of the pain in my back."

The wiry youth sitting next to Camacho told me he knew he would have back trouble when he was older if he kept using the short hoe. "It happens to everyone," he said. "Using it hurts so bad, the *mayordomo* brings beer at lunch so we will work in the *pinche* afternoon. The beer helps a little. Instead of drinking beer, some of the *vatos* smoke *mota* to make it *por la tarde*."[1]

Through the evening, I listened. Héctor finally said, "*Abogado*,[2] I realize you're very busy in your office, but I have a friend. He's a farm labor contractor. Maybe he will let you join his crew to see how it is using the *cortito*. It will help you understand our problem."

I didn't respond.

"You're new here, *abogado*," Héctor reminded me. "You say you came to work for CRLA because you want to do something for farm workers. I hope you stay. But if you really want to help us, you will get rid of the *cortito*. I was a farm worker when I came to the United States. I liked doing farm work, but ten years ago I found a different kind of work because it was too painful working with the short hoe. I swore someday I would get it outlawed."

With his pea-green shirt hanging outside his creased gray pants, Héctor leaned over, sliding the cue between his thumb and forefinger ready to break the waiting balls for a final game of eight ball. A *norteño* accordion blasted from an unseen jukebox. Watching the pool balls scatter, I considered Héctor's request that I try working with the short hoe. *I don't have to bend over all day to understand the problem*, I thought.

Before leaving the *cantina*, I accepted Héctor's challenge. "At least I'll be working outside, and it can't be that hard," I said to Héctor while we walked to our cars. "I'm in good shape from surfing."

---

[1] The term *mayordomo* is Spanish for "supervisor"; and *mota* is Spanish slang for "marijuana". *Por la tarde* is Spanish for "in the afternoon" or "early evening."
[2] *Abogado* is Spanish for "lawyer."

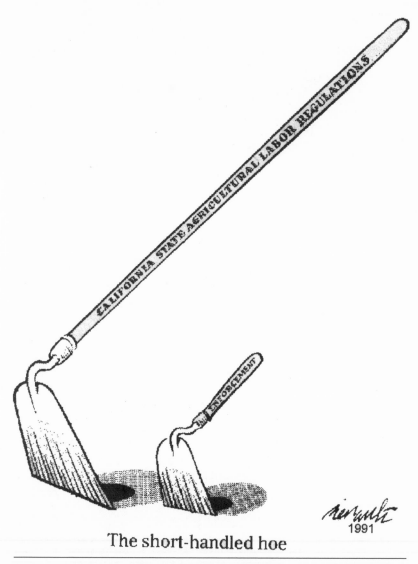

The short-handled hoe

The agribusiness industry showed its dominance by forcing farm workers to stoop in the hot dusty field, raising and lowering the *cortito* from dawn to dusk to do work that could be done with a normal hoe. (Courtesy of Dennis Renault, *The Sacramento Bee,* 1991)

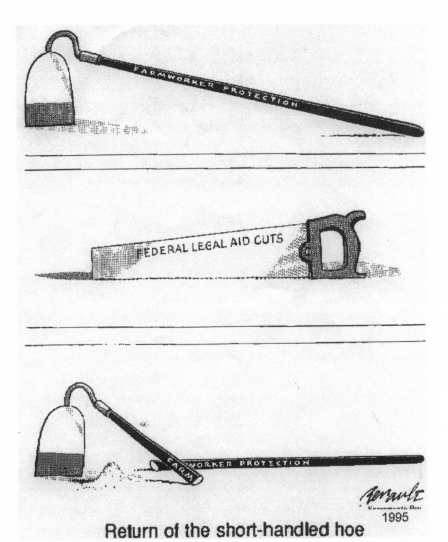

Return of the short-handled hoe

When the federal government drastically reduced funds to legal service programs, such as CRLA, farm workers were left with little or no protection. (Courtesy of Dennis Renault, *The Sacramento Bee,* 1995)

Two

It was still dark Saturday morning when I pulled over on the dirt shoulder beside the southern Salinas Valley sugar-beet field. I was about to spend the day doing stoop labor. Héctor and a muscular companion in his mid-forties climbed down from the back of the farm labor contractor's new 1969 GMC pickup.

"Héctor tells me you want to work with us for a few days," said the dark-eyed contractor.

"I'll try." I yawned, sliding from the driver's seat in faded Levi's, a tattered Stanford sweatshirt, and brown rough-out boots.

"Why does a lawyer want to work?" asked the contractor, grinning.

I shrugged. "Some clients think if I use the short hoe for a few days, I'll understand a legal problem we talked about."

"Don't be afraid to be honest with me, my friend," said the farm labor contractor, his piercing eyes barely visible under the brim of his black cowboy hat. "Héctor told me what he wants you to do."

I looked down, a child caught with his hand in the cookie jar. The contractor continued. "Héctor is fighting a windmill. Getting rid of the short-handled hoe is impossible. You working in the field for a few days won't change that, but who am I to stop you. Here's a hoe. I'll pay you the same as I pay the others, a dollar thirty-five an hour."

By eight, before the sun broke through the gunmetal overcast, I was ready to quit. Knife slashes of pain penetrated my lower back. My right shoulder throbbed. Stopping on his way from the portable toilet, Héctor watched me, bent to the ground, slowly thinning the four-inch-high plants with the short-handled hoe, leaving them eight-to-ten inches apart. "How do you feel, Mo?" he asked.

6

"Fucked," I grimaced.

Héctor smiled and walked on.

By nine, the mustached contractor, whose neatly tucked shirt looked like it had just left the cleaners, yelled at me when I repeatedly stood upright, rubbing my lower back. "Lawyer, if you can't keep up, you can quit."

I looked to my right and saw the thirty-worker crew a quarter-mile ahead. Their bent bodies moved briskly down the half-mile-long rows.

At noon, while the other stoop laborers sat in the sun eating tacos and drinking cold Pepsi or beer, I lay unable to move in the shade of my Volkswagen bus. When work resumed at one, I remained inert. My shoulder and lower back pulsed like a migraine headache with hard-rock music ready to resume. The farm labor contractor stopped above me. "It's time to get back to work, *abogado*. Is the work we do too hard for a city boy?"

I looked up. Héctor walked over, took my left hand, and pulled me to my feet. Shuffling to the rows to be thinned, I dreaded picking up a short hoe. Slowly leaning over, I recalled the pain I felt once in a high school football game. I was playing outside linebacker, ready to tackle a running back coming around my end, when out of nowhere the left knee of a monster tackle hit me between the legs. The running back shot by and I lay on the grass in agony. *Getting kneed between the legs hurt*, I thought, *but the pain came and went. Bending over with the* cortito *is nonstop pain. This is different. Have I done anything that hurts as much as using the short hoe?*

I recalled once walking with my mother into a doctor's office when I was eleven. I had an earache that shot a piercing pain through the left side of my head. I tried to tell the doctor that for a week I had a cold and my runny nose turned into an earache. He wouldn't listen. He decided my problem was impacted wax, so for half an hour a nurse armed with a pump, tube, and nozzle sprayed hot water at high pressure into my already painful ear. *The high-pressure water hurt*, I thought, *but this was different*. At the doctor's office I just laid there in constant pain. Now, every time I bent over an inch closer to the ground or rose an inch further from the ground, or twisted to the right, or twisted to the left, a sharp pain penetrated my lower back.

In the field near King City, I stood with the short hoe in my hand, knowing that unlike the eleven-year-old who couldn't force the doctor not to torture his patients, I could avoid the pain merely by telling Héctor that I had used the short hoe enough to understand the seriousness of his problem. But etched in my memory were the thousands of stooped farm workers I had seen in fields across the state. They could not just stand up and walk away.

As the sun slid over the coastal hills five hours later, I dropped the *cortito* that by then seemed to weigh far more than its two pounds and shuffled from the field. Reluctantly, I promised Héctor I would return on Monday.

Three

ON THE RIDE HOME, the thrill of lurking opportunity was lost in the pain piercing my right shoulder. I limped into my Salinas office and found my law school classmate Ralph Abascal there alone. When I told him about the short-handled hoe, he reminded me that workers who are injured on the job must obtain relief through workers' compensation. They cannot go directly to court. A private attorney would represent an injured worker without charging a fee. As his fee, the attorney would receive part of whatever the worker was awarded for his or her injury. The federal government that provided California Rural Legal Assistance with funds did not permit us to take cases a private attorney would handle without charging the client a fee. I had to refer a workers' compensation case to a private lawyer.

"Oh, man," I responded, "I wish I would have thought of that before I spent all day stooped in the field."

While I expressed regret in responding to Abascal, my feelings were mixed. I wanted to stop the suffering of stooped farm workers, but I didn't look forward to undergoing the pain of stooping all day over a short-handled hoe. Abascal shrugged his bulky shoulders. "The only way you can handle the case is if private lawyers won't take it for some reason."

Around midnight I called Héctor. "I'm going to refer Carmona's case to a private lawyer. A workers' compensation specialist will get him more money than I could."

"He doesn't want money, *abogado*. I thought you were going to get rid of stoop labor."

"Will you tell your friend I won't be there Monday?" I asked meekly.

"So you're not going to help Carmona and his friends?"

I hesitated. "Thank the contractor for me. He doesn't have to pay me anything."

"I guess you don't have time to try to get the *cortito* outlawed. You're lucky you're a lawyer, not a farm worker," Héctor said bitterly into the phone.

"I understand why you want to get rid of the short hoe. No one should have to do that work."

"Farm workers in Soledad have no choice. We do what the boss tells us to do. We have to feed our families. You let us down."

"I can't represent farm workers in the short-handled hoe case."

"You're not going to help, like you promised?"

"I want to, but I can't."

"I thought you were different, *abogado*. But you're like all the rest. You make a promise and you don't follow through."

Four

FOR ME, walking the sometimes adventurous, sometimes lonely roads of California's fields started late one 1967 afternoon during my second year of law school. The young woman I lived with, Kathy, a classmate Ralph Abascal, and I rode down the peninsula from a San Francisco antiwar march. We had just left friends in Haight-Ashbury who were planning their parts in what would come to be known as the "summer of love."

In 1967, it seemed to me and my buddies that kids in the San Francisco Bay area had three options: go to Haight-Ashbury and smoke dope, go to the streets and fight for what we called justice, or go to Santa Cruz and ride waves. I had been riding waves for more than half my life. I was older but not too different than the eager fifteen-year-old who bought his first balsa surfboard for forty dollars. Even though my hair covered my collar, like most of my surfing friends, I always worked and didn't make smoking marijuana part of my life. That's what we felt distinguished us from most of the Haight-Ashbury residents. But I have to admit I liked to sit on the curb in Haight-Ashbury watching the world pass by. I felt close to, but not quite part of, Haight-Ashbury. My bushy hair reflected my lack of concern about how others saw me. I knew strangers would continue to consider me a hippie no matter what I did. I liked the idea of fighting for justice. I was against the war in Vietnam, I was angry that the silent majority believed African-Americans inherently less competent than Whites (except in sports and music), and I supported the brown-skinned farm workers' struggle.

"So what are you gonna do this summer?" Abascal asked.

"Work for the public defender in Orange County." When he

looked at me, I added, "So I can surf after work."

"Want to work with farm workers? Some lawyers are coming from their East Coast ivy-league schools to set up law offices. They're fighting the War on Poverty."

"What's the War on Poverty?"

"President Johnson's New Deal. He told Congress that poverty is a domestic enemy that threatens our nation. He declared war on poverty. Want to work with the poverty lawyers helping farm workers?"

I laughed. "I know farm workers have a hard life, but I don't owe them a summer of mine. I'm not gonna suffer all summer away from the ocean so I can help some New England do-gooders fight a war that can't be won."

"Jourdane, all you've ever done is lifeguard. You need to try working in an office. You're gonna be a lawyer next year."

"I'm not going to law school so I can represent farm workers."

Abascal suggested I read John Steinbeck's *Grapes of Wrath* and then decide.

Kathy and I ended up spending the summer in Delano. The federal government had placed the California Rural Legal Assistance office at a crossroads a few miles south of Delano called McFarland because the ongoing dispute between César Chávez and the grape growers in Delano had given the small town of Delano a negative political aura. One evening, we went to visit the Del Valle family, clients in the Sunset Camp near the southern end of the San Joaquin Valley. The family was being evicted from the camp because the parents of four young girls would let only the oldest, a fifteen-year-old, work in the fields during the summer. The other daughters were being encouraged to advance their education by attending summer school.

Walking from the edge of the road between Arvin and Lamont where we parked Kathy's Impala, we saw the farm workers' homes planted on harsh gray dirt. "They're Quonset huts," Kathy whispered. "It looks more like a prisoner-of-war camp than a place to raise little girls." Holding hands like newlyweds, we crossed the dusty field. Ahead lay rows of identical metal boxes. All were drab olive-green, lined up in the barren landscape—not a blade of grass or seedling choking its way through the parched earth. The home of the clients we were visiting, like all the others, had no front door. Just a rusty screen covered the entrance to the one-room hovel. I knocked on the wall adjacent to the torn screen.

We were greeted by a young Latina teenager wearing Levi's and a blue work shirt, her hair partially covered by a red and black bandana.

"Is your father or mother home?" I asked.

Like tears, perspiration ran down the dark-haired girl's brown cheeks. Looking down, she told us her father was called into work the night shift. She invited us in. A single lightbulb hung naked from the corrugated-steel ceiling. Three neatly made mattresses covered all but a small corner of the cracked cement floor. An old single-burner stove stood in one corner; an ice chest rested on the mattress in another. There was no sink, no kitchen counter, no refrigerator.

Inside the farm worker's home we met the girl's mother. Kathy and I could not turn down the steaming beans and cheese wrapped in fresh tortillas she offered after we introduced ourselves. Standing in the tiny room, we enjoyed the delicious Mexican food, using a wrinkled brown paper bag as a napkin. When bean juice dripped from my napkin onto the white concrete floor, Kathy pulled a handkerchief from her rear pocket and wiped the brown spots. Apparently feeling self-conscious, she looked out the window toward the shade of her parked sedan. "The beans are good," she said with a full mouth. "It's pretty hot in here. Why don't we talk outside?"

"You met my daughter?" the *señora* asked in Spanish.

"Yes, I guess," I replied in my high school Spanish, extending my hand to the attractive Latina. I wanted to add but had not yet learned the words to say, "She answered our knock. I guess I assumed she was your daughter."

While I licked refried pinto beans from my fingers, the *señora* told me about her problem, speaking very slowly in Spanish. After a while, Kathy overcame her modesty and asked the girl if there was somewhere she could wash her hands. "I'm sorry, *señora*, but we do not have a bathroom inside," the girl responded. Pointing to a public washroom across the dirt road, she added, "We must go over there."

When Kathy began to walk toward the army-green building, the young Latina joined her. "I'll show you where the women's room door is," she said softly.

Displaying my lack of experience with life in farm labor camps, I asked Señora Del Valle, "You don't have running water inside your home?"

"No, *Señor abogado*. It gives us shame, so we do not have visitors from outside the camp."

Near eleven, we said good evening to Señora Del Valle. On the ride back to our apartment, Kathy and I talked about the farm workers' life I was seeing for the first time.

"Yet, did you see those kids playing?" I asked. "Shooting marbles and laughing in the hot dust like they were playing Marco Polo in a country club swimming pool."

Kathy smiled.

"Did you see the three pictures hanging on the wall above the bed?" I asked.

"The felt ones of Christ, JFK, and César Chávez?"

"Yeah. I understand having pictures of Jesus Christ and President Kennedy. I need to learn more about César Chávez. While you were with the girl, Mrs. Del Valle and I talked about him. She sees César Chávez as the hope for her children's future. She said if his union represented the workers in her camp, the manager would never have tried to evict her family for merely seeking to better the lives of her young daughters. Chávez would have had ten thousand workers marching outside the camp entrance."

An attorney in our office, Bill Daniels, later told me the Sunset Camp was the government camp where the Joad family found freedom from the dangerous makeshift settlements in Steinbeck's *Grapes of Wrath*.

'It's Good To See Young Folks Working Within The System.'

Before César Chávez, Dolores Huerta, and the United Farm Workers, thousands of Mexican-American children spent their summers working in the fields doing the same strenuous work that adults did. (Courtesy of Dennis Renault, *The Sacramento Bee,* 1972)

Five

ON INDEPENDENCE DAY, Kathy and I went to a farm workers' celebration in Delano's central park. Along the edge of the weed-plagued grass, we walked hand in hand like two young kids walking in a Kansas or Missouri summer. The towering eucalyptus trees shielded us from the burning midday sun. The aroma of *carne asada* and *carnitas* captured my senses and made me hungry. From a makeshift stage near the corner of the park blared the electric guitars, horns, and drums of a Tijuana-sounding band. Almost every man wore a neatly tucked white shirt with rolled-up sleeves and open collar. The farm workers talked in groups of four or five, their combined voices buzzing like a band saw broken by deep laughter. Chunky women in colorful dresses or full skirts gossiped over cement picnic tables while they shucked corn. Between the tables young children ran, playing chase. Their older brothers played soccer in an open area; their older sisters sat in groups watching the older brothers. Seeing the people in the park reminded me that until 1845, not long before the discovery of gold in California flooded the state with Easterners, California was part of Mexico.

At the festival, we saw Gil Flores, with whom I worked, and met a young man who had come to the United States from Mexico years earlier with a permit to work in the fields under the U.S. government's and Mexico's Bracero Program—a guest-worker program. In Spanish, *bracero* means one who uses his arms. Braceros were manual laborers imported from Mexico. In the latter half of the nineteenth century, tens of thousands of Mexicans came to California to do farm work. Over the years, although people of all nationalities joined them, they continued to be the predominant farm labor force in California.

Complaints by the Mexican workers in the 1920s led to Mexican President Venustiano Carranza drafting a model contract that guaranteed Mexican workers in the United States rights in the Mexican constitution, identified employers, and set pay rates and work schedules before the Mexicans were given permission to leave Mexico. In 1924, the U.S. Border Patrol was established and the concept of "illegal aliens" commenced. With World War II and a claimed labor shortage, the United States and Mexico entered the Bracero Treaty.

Under the Bracero Treaty, between 1942 and 1965, over 4.5 million braceros entered the United States, most as farm workers. While World War II and the labor shortage it caused were claimed as the reasons for the need to import farm workers, the Bracero Program continued after the war ended, and, of the 4.5 million braceros imported between 1942 and 1965, less than 200,000 came during the war. During the 1950s, with the war and the claimed labor shortage over, around two million braceros came to work in the fields in the United States. In the early 1960s, with growing pressure from scholars like Ernesto Galarza and George I. Sánchez, and the incipient labor movement being led by César Chávez, President Kennedy's secretary of labor, W. Willard Wirtz, made it more and more difficult for the agribusiness industry to obtain permission to import braceros. Eventually, in 1964, through growing opposition by liberal senators and members of Congress, the Bracero Program was brought to an end.

According to Kitty Calavita in *Inside the State*, while the social pressure to eliminate the Bracero Program was abetted with the increased use of machines in some fields, especially cotton fields in Texas, the growers' hopes for continued cheap labor lay in a provision in section 101, subdivision (a)(1)(H)(ii) of the Immigration and Naturalization Act of 1952. Under the subdivision, known as H-2, temporary aliens could be brought into the United States if there was a certified labor shortage.[1] Between 1952 and 1964, thousands of aliens were imported under subdivision H-2 to do farm work; but under an executive agreement, while the Bracero Program was in effect, Mexi-

---

[1] *Inside the State: The Bracero Program, Immigration, and the I.N.S.* (New York: Routledge, 1992).

can workers were excluded from subdivision H-2. With the formal end of the Bracero Program in December 1964, workers from Mexico continued to come to the United States as what former CRLA director Marty Glick called *de facto* braceros. If a grower obtained a labor shortage certificate he could bring in Mexicans to do fieldwork in California. As a result, California growers continued to operate as if the Bracero Program were still in effect. In consolidated lawsuits filed in federal court during the summer of 1967, Glick, Bob Gnaizda, and Sheldon Green, another California Rural Legal Assistance attorney working in Modesto, presented evidence that *de facto* braceros were being brought into the United States although there was an abundance of resident farm workers available to do the work being taken by the imported workers.

As the Delano holiday festival forged on around us, Kathy, my colleague, Gil Flores, and I spoke at length to the young Mexican field laborer we met there. He appeared to be in his early twenties. Between the young farm worker's limited English and Gil's and Kathy's Spanish, I eventually succeeded in informing the young man that Gil and I worked with lawyers who were trying to stop the growers from importing *de facto* braceros under the H-2 provisions that seemed to extend the exploitation of Mexican workers.

"*Chale*," the youth said angrily. "If you do that, I will not be able to come legally to the United States and work."

I sat petrified and wordless, realizing I had threatened the young Mexican worker.

"The grower I work for says he'll be forced out of business if he can't get workers from Mexico," the young man reported. "He says people who live here would rather receive welfare than do farm work."

"No way," Kathy said in Spanish. "They just don't want to pay enough so you can buy food and pay rent." Kathy grew up in Fresno. Her parents grew crops on their Merced and West San Joaquin Valley acreage. She learned Spanish from workers on her parents' farms, working beside them in the packing shed every summer.

The young farm worker admitted there were problems with the Bracero Program; even though the growers needed workers from

Mexico, they made them stay many days in a crowded camp in Mexico until someone in the United States requested them for employment purposes. "When I leave Michoacán in the spring it is cool," he said. "The sky is clear. The buds are bursting on the hillside. The air is fresh. The camp they took us to is near the border. It was hot and there was much dust in the air. The food was bad. There was little water. If we did not want to be there for long time, we had to give a *mordida*. . . ."

"What's *mordida*?" I asked, reminded that I had to learn more Spanish.

"It is a, *cómo se dice*. . . ."

"A bribe," said Kathy.

"*Gracias, señora*. I saved fifty American dollars each year from my pay to give *mordidas* when I returned the next year. Those who do not have money for the *mordida* have to wait many weeks to come."

"That's why union organizers and the people I work with want to end the Bracero Program. Now the lawyers I work with say it continues but they just call it a different name," I said.

Again the youth stared at us with confusion growing in his dark eyes.

Realizing we should move the conversation to more secure ground, Kathy asked the teenager what he did.

"Pick."

"How much do they pay?" I asked.

"Not much, but at home we earn only thirty *pesos* for one day working."

"Thirty *pesos* is only two-and-a-half dollars in American money," I said, "and picking is hard work, isn't it?"

"Very hard work, yes. We earn more in your country, but you make us work faster than we do in Mexico."

"Long hours, too?" I asked.

The youth told us he started work before the sun came up and continued until dark. After he left the camp in Mexico, he worked in the Coachella Valley. He said that from the field he could see the Cadillacs speed by taking the rich to Palm Springs to play golf. When the picking was finished in Coachella, he came north if he picked fast enough. If not, they said he was lazy and sent him back to Mexico.

"That's why farm workers need a union," said Kathy.

"But if the company learns I want the union, they will send me back to Mexico no matter how fast I pick," responded the former bracero.

"If it's so bad, why do you come?" I asked.

"If I do not work, I have no money to go to school in the winter. Without school, I will be a laborer all my life."

"But it's pretty hot working in the sun all day," I said.

"*Usted sabe, señor,* every day it is like today, almost 40 centigrade, 100 of your degrees."

While Kathy, Gil, and I talked with the young farm worker, a short, dark man with Native-American features walked up in a lime-green, short-sleeve shirt and baggy beige pants. He asked the farm worker, "Did I overhear you say you don't want to be a farm laborer when you are older?"

"*Sí, señor.* It pays very little and it is a very low job."

"But, you grow and harvest the food people all over the world must have to live. If you were paid what is fair for your work and given the respect you deserve, would you feel different about doing farm work?"

"*Sí, señor.* I like working outside more than sitting in a room adding the numbers or typing the papers, but the growers will never pay what is fair or respect us for what we do."

Watching the stranger listen so attentively to the teen, I glanced at his eyes and saw total focus on the young man's every word.

The dark stranger extended his hand to the farm worker. "What you say is true," he said. "With others like you, we will make farm work a respected career."

The stranger nodded to Gil Flores, telling me without words that they were well acquainted, and then he turned to me. He extended his hand and asked if I was the summer law student at California Rural Legal Assistance.

"Uh huh," I replied.

"My name is César Chávez," the stranger said. Suddenly, a slight-framed older man whose gray hair blew in the hot breeze and a bulkier and younger but already balding man plowed through the sea of playing children. Both were dressed, like most of the farm workers in the park, in plain shirts and baggy trousers. The elder told Chávez they had to talk. When the three walked away, the bulkier man chattered to the union leader like a chipmunk.

I later learned that the one talking to Chávez was Jerry Cohen, the union's lawyer. The other was Fred Ross of the Community Service Organization (CSO). Ross came to California to help workers. He was looking for a local leader to help extend his organizing efforts to the agricultural sector when a priest in San Jose told him about Chávez, then a budding organizer in San Jose's Sal Si Puedes neighborhood. Ross went to Sal Si Puedes to meet Chávez. Sal Si Puedes, Spanish for "leave if you can," was one of the City of San Jose's largest and poorest Mexican-American communities. For days, Ross tried to talk with Chávez, but César avoided him. Too many white students writing their doctoral theses had been coming from area universities to Sal Si Puedes to ask the Mexicans endless questions: Why do your children score so low on intelligence tests? Why do your children do worse in school than white children? And do you believe beans and tortillas for breakfast interfere with your children's ability to learn? Ross, however, was unrelenting in his pursuit of Chávez. He simply would not take no for an answer.

When Chávez finally agreed to meet Ross, he also invited a group of tough punks from the neighborhood to join the discussion, hoping to scare off the *gringo*. It didn't. Fred Ross had been organizing on the streets of Chicago for twenty years. He knew what it took to be a leader. Seeing Chávez control the hoodlums who surrounded him and hearing him softly express anger about farm workers' working conditions convinced Ross that he'd found the person he'd been searching for. He tried to hire Chávez but, again, César refused. Fred Ross, being a union organizer, still wouldn't give up. Eventually, after much cajoling by Ross, César agreed to go to Oxnard for a year to help the CSO educate farm workers and register them to vote.

When Fred Ross and César Chávez returned to the table where we sat, Ross apologized for interrupting us. Chávez began to explain to the farm worker youth that without the Bracero or H-2 Program, the young man and his friends could apply for immigrant visas and return to the United States to work freely in the fields they chose, with a union contract. Under these circumstances, Chávez told the youth, he and those from his homeland would no longer be herded like cattle into a feedlot, waiting for the boss to come and select workers, as if choosing white-faced Herefords to slaughter. The young farm worker listened intently to the dark-featured man who with so few words had painted a detailed illustration he could understand concerning the need for an agricultural labor union.

Turning to me, Chávez said, "I'm glad you're here. We have many legal problems but little money to hire lawyers to solve them."

"I've heard a lot about you, Mr. Chávez. You are doing much for farm workers," I responded.

"My name is César," replied Chávez, his youthful smile revealing his modesty.

"Were you a farm worker?" I asked.

"Most of my life. I started when I was eleven. We lost our property in Yuma, Arizona, during the Depression. We migrated to California and moved from company to company seeking work."

"I guess that's what brought a lot of workers to California," I said, recalling John Steinbeck's *Grapes of Wrath* and the Joad family. "That's what Steinbeck wrote about, people losing their land to the bank in Oklahoma."

"Now, it is the children of the families from Oklahoma who treat us the worst."

"Why do migrants from Oklahoma feel such contempt toward migrants from Mexico?" I asked. Before Chávez responded, I thought, what a dumb question. My mind filled with a picture of the 1600s when poor whites from England came to America to work as indentured servants for rich Virginia tobacco growers. The indentured servants came to America hoping one day to become rich tobacco growers themselves. But after they were freed from the servitude, they had no money to buy land near the fertile Virginia coast, so they moved inland to settle on free or cheap land. They became the frontiersmen. The problem was, the land they moved onto belonged to Indian tribes. The poor whites killed poorer Indians who resisted their invasion. And, later, in the West, the poor whites from Oklahoma fought the poorer migrants from Mexico who took their jobs.

Chávez reminded me that John Steinbeck showed the world how in the 1930s the agribusiness establishment ruthlessly abused the workers who happened to be Dust Bowl refugees. "At least when President Roosevelt was in the White House," Chávez added, "he provided government camps as safe havens for those who most needed it."

"Unlike many politicians today," Kathy said, "he cared about the common people. Now, the government is closing the camps."

Chávez told us that the growers needed farm workers in the summer to pick their grapes and peaches, "but they do not want their children here in the winter contaminating the schools attended by their white children. When the harvest is over each year, those in power treat immigrants, whether they come from Mexico or Oklahoma, like rotting dinner scraps they want to discard after consuming the best part."

"I guess they forget that none of us would be here were it not for some brave immigrant in our family tree," I said.

"If we forget the inscription on the base of the Statue of Liberty," Chávez said, "and neglect those who leave their homeland and migrate to California because they are hungry, we can no longer hold our heads up with pride."

"A lot of my classmates think it would be better for citizens who pay taxes if we quit giving so many benefits to immigrants," I said.

"And today's law students are tomorrow's legislators," Chávez said, slowly shaking his head. "Will California deny health care to a sick little girl because her family members are immigrants? Will we refuse to nourish and educate the hungry immigrant child? Your office sees many immigrants. Will the lawyers working there tomorrow refuse to help those in need because they are not citizens?"

"I hope the day never comes when we take that unforgivable step backwards," I responded. "I've seen a lot of immigrants this summer, but worse than being an immigrant is stooping over all day in the hot sun. It might be the only way to do the job, but my heart races every time I see the bent bodies."

Chávez nodded. "Like so many, I wake up in the night with the pain that comes from stooping in the field all day. The short hoe is the nail they use to hang us from the cross. Someday the union will do something about it, but right now we're fighting for survival."

Chávez told us he had just learned that the workers at a large ranch were ready to strike. His union had only one lawyer. Chávez told us that if a strike erupted, the workers' problems would multiply. Workers' cars would be repossessed when they had no paycheck to make their monthly payment. Workers would be evicted from their homes when they had no paycheck to pay their rent. The doctors who cared for a worker's children and the corner grocer who provided the children with bread and milk would not silently wait for payment just because the farm worker had chosen to strike.

After others drew Chávez away, Kathy, Gil, and I talked about why people followed him. "I mean he seems nice," I said, "but so are lots of people."

"He communicates with everyone. He listens to the poorest and least educated farm workers with the same attention he listens to the governor," Gil replied. "Without using big words or making promises like a politician, he explains what he's doing, and people line up to help him. Maybe he's so effective a leader because he read about Ghandi and learned."

César's warning was accurate. Not long after the celebration in Delano's park, I read in the *Bakersfield Californian* that a strike had erupted across the county because the companies were refusing to recognize César Chávez and his farm workers' union. During the lunch hour on day two of the strike, I was sitting in the CRLA office behind the receptionist's desk when an attractive Latina wearing a red T-shirt and faded Levi's stormed into our storefront office.

"Let me see a lawyer," she demanded.

"None are here," I responded, already intimidated.

"Where are they?"

"At hearings or something. Can I help you?"

"Who are you?" she asked me.

"A law student here for the summer."

"Come with me, law student. We need you at the picket line. The cops are going crazy."

"I can't leave," I pleaded. "I promised I'd watch the office."

The young woman grabbed my hand. "Come on," she demanded. "It's siesta time. No one's coming to your empty office now."

Feeling the soft fingers of the young woman who sounded so powerful demolished my will to resist. She was only a few years older than me, slightly smaller, and had a perfectly molded sun-darkened face; but her intimidating air caused me to feel more like a criminal led from the courtroom to a jail cell than a college student led onto a dance floor.

Passing by rows of grapevines, we rode south in one of the battered white Dodge Darts all United Farm Workers organizers seemed to drive. In California, the vehicle one drives is as reflective of the driver as clothing or hairstyle. Almost everyone has a car or truck. This was equally true in the late 1960s. Then, unlike Southern California, where Thunderbird and Corvette convertibles prevailed, or the Bay Area, where BMWs and Audis were preferred, the UFW's white Dodge Darts were most plentiful on the roads and highways crossing the barren California fields. Typically, they could be seen passing occasional older Chevys and Ford pickup trucks with farm workers behind the wheel.

"I didn't catch your name," I said to the young lady driving.

"Dolores," replied the woman as she raced down the flat country road.

"Dolores Huerta?"

She nodded.

"You've been with Chávez for a long time."

"Since we started," she answered.

"Are you from Delano?"

"You ask a lot of questions." She turned to look at me. "You sound like a lawyer already."

Passing a slow-moving old Ford and narrowly missing an oncoming truck loaded with melons, Dolores told me she was reared in Stockton. Her mother housed migrant farm workers. She grew up seeing how they were treated in the fields and yearned to better their lives. Her mother spent the little they had not on herself but on tuition and books so Dolores could become a teacher for children of farm workers who attended school hungry and needed shoes.

"A teacher?" I asked.

Huerta told me she started to teach but Fred Ross convinced her to work for CSO.

When I told her I'd learned recently that CSO stood for the Community Service Organization, she looked at me with approval. Dolores said she had met César and his wife Helen in the CSO. The three had been together ever since then.

Dolores and César were convinced the workers had to have a union if they were going to improve their lives. When the CSO decided to spend most of its efforts on voter registration to elect representatives who would help farm workers instead of organizing the workers to help themselves, Dolores and César started the National Farm Workers Association. They moved to Delano and began holding house meetings to explain to workers how a union could improve their lives. Dolores told me that around the same time, Larry Itliong had started a union for farm workers in the Stockton area. César's union was made up mostly of Mexicans. Itliong's members were Filipinos. In the spring of 1965, César's union supported Itliong's strike at McFarland Rose Company. During the following months the strike spread. Five thousand workers walked off the job and the Delano grape strike began. In 1966 the two unions merged and became the United Farm Workers (UFW). That year, they signed an important initial contract with the Schenley Wine Company. "César wants [us] to be part of the AFL-CIO someday," Dolores added to her brief history lesson as we rode through the grape fields, "and we will be the United Farm Workers, AFL-CIO."

In a cloud of dust that engulfed the striking farm workers carrying "*Huelga*" (or "On Strike") signs, three sheriff's cars sped away in front of us on the road's dirt shoulder. Dolores pulled over and the workers immediately surrounded the Dodge Dart.

"*Al fin,*[1] you made it," shouted a dark-skinned youth, perspiration

---

[1]The term *Al fin* is Spanish for "finally."

soaking his long-sleeved shirt in the 108-degree sun. "Did you bring help?"

"I brought a witness."

The farm worker looked at me and scoffed. "A *pinchi güero* kid?"[2]

"He was all I could find," she responded.

"Ms. Huerta told me that she came to our law office after she saw patrol cars arrive," I said, trying to sound like an attorney.

The farm worker stared into my eyes. I could feel him trying to determine whether I was worth talking to.

"We were just yelling at the scabs," he finally said. Carrying guns and batons, the sheriffs screamed at the strikers to leave or be arrested. "They scared some of the *carnales* away.[3] They pushed Yolanda down into the vines when she demanded their names. They forced her arms behind her back so they could lock her in handcuffs."

"Did they arrest anyone else?" Dolores asked.

"No. I told the cops, like you told me, we have a right to be here," the young farm worker replied. "They just stormed off with Yolanda in the rear seat, telling us to be gone before they return."

"Wasn't Yolanda's daughter with her?" Dolores countered.

"They took her, too. I think they said they were taking her to juvy."

"Juvenile hall?"

"*Simón.*"[4]

"Let me get Cohen," Dolores said. "We need a lawyer."

Dolores started for the car. "Come on, law student. I need to use a phone. I'll take you back to your lonely office."

That summer, César and Dolores challenged the agribusiness industry on a wide scale with a "kitchen cabinet" of dedicated companions comparable to those surrounding FDR during the 1930s—a group including César's brothers Richard and Manuel, Esther and Gilbert Padilla, Larry Itliong and Phillip Veracruz, Marshall Ganz,

---

[2]*Güero* is Spanish slang for "white-" or "light-skinned."
[3]*Carnales* is the Spanish equivalent of the English slang term "Homies."
[4]*Simón* is Spanish slang for "yes" or "correct."

Jessica Govea, Diana and Mack Lyons, the Reverend Chris Hartmire from the Migrant Ministry, Leroy Chatfield, Carlos and Linda Le-Gerrette, and Jerry Cohen. Meanwhile, through a rural lawyer's office, working under Gary Bellow, Bill Daniels, and Kenny Hegland, I spent the hot days focusing on the snares rigged against farm workers in their daily lives. I tried to prevent evictions from their homes, repossession of their cars, and garnishment of their paychecks. In effect, I spent my days trying to put together pieces of the farm workers' often unsolvable legal puzzle.

Six

WHEN I RETURNED TO SAN FRANCISCO for my third year of law school, I was overwhelmed by the farm workers' working conditions I had seen over the summer. I was inspired by the efforts of César Chávez and Dolores Huerta to improve those conditions. I wrote a law review article entitled the "Constitutionality of the Exclusion of Farm Workers from the National Labor Relations Act," and a year later I started a permanent job with the CRLA office in Salinas.

After completing the state bar exam, Kathy and I loaded all our belongings into the blue Volkswagen bus I had just purchased for $500 and moved down the coast to Salinas, a hundred miles south of San Francisco. Salinas is nestled ten miles inland from cypress-lined Monterey Bay in a wide valley between rolling hills, the Santa Lucia Mountains, and Los Padres National Forest. The annual highlight in the areas surrounding Steinbeck's *East of Eden, Of Mice and Men,* and *Red Pony* is Big Week, which includes the largest rodeo in the West. When Kathy and I arrived, the less-than-100,000 population of the Salinas Valley was about half middle-class Anglos, half impoverished Mexican immigrants, and a sprinkling of Filipinos, African-Americans, Japanese-Americans, and more well-off descendants of long-ago Mexican and Anglo settlers.

The Salinas Valley stretches from Moss Landing in the North to San Ardo in the South, encasing Castroville, Salinas, Spreckles, Chular, Gonzalez, Soledad, Greenfield, and King City. It is California's spread-out version of Brooklyn with the San Francisco Bay Area as its Manhattan Island. Unlike Brooklyn with its earlier-day Jewish immigrants who faced the rough North Atlantic packed into human-cargo freighters, later replaced by Puerto Ricans, many of the early-day residents in the Salinas Valley were from Oklahoma and Arkansas and had arrived in the promised land in overheated and over-packed model T's trying to escape the Dust Bowl and bank foreclosures of their family farms. They were replaced by immigrant farm workers from Mexico during World War II and, up until 1964, by braceros. But Mexican-Americans, Filipinos, Arabs, and others had worked the fields across the Salinas Valley since the nineteenth century.

After passing Woolworth's, Montgomery Wards, and Foster Freeze on the morning following Labor Day, I waited at a Main Street crosswalk, watching Levi-clad students carrying books to their Salinas High School classes. *This could be Tulsa or Cheyenne,* I thought. *Why did I talk myself into coming here?*

My concern for workers in California's fields started at my grandparents' small farm in rural San Diego County. My grandfather grew avocados and grapefruit. My grandmother cared for a fat cow, squawking ducks, an overweight spotted dog, and peach trees. For a month or so every summer, my older sister and my younger brothers and I explored the rolling hills or the chaparral-lined creek. One morning while we were hunting for crawdads in the knee-deep rivulet running alongside a narrow country road that is now the freeway, Highway 78, two older Mexican guys emerged from the dense cottonwoods. They looked like teenagers who had slept for weeks in their baggy khakis and stained white shirts. One yelled to us in Spanish.

"What?" I yelled back.

The stranger again yelled something in Spanish, slower this time.

"We don't understand Spanish," yelled my brother John.

The black-haired youths looked at each other, shrugged their shoulders, crossed the creeks and headed off through the tall grass. That evening, I told grandpa about seeing the Mexicans. The gray-haired elder sat us down on the skimpy grass patch outside the kitchen under the saucer-peach tree. Dinner's fried-chicken aroma lingered in the humid summer air while my grandfather spoke. "Forty years ago," he told us, "I chased Pancho Villa across Texas and Mexico. He may have been Mexico's George Washington but to the U.S. Army he was a cattle rustler. I was a private in the U.S. Army and I followed orders. Now I rely on Mexicans to pick my fruit. No one ever worked so hard. They sleep in the field so they can send most of the money they earn to their families in Mexico. They have been forced to leave their family in Mexico and come to America to earn a living."

The next morning at breakfast, Grandpa began teaching us enough Spanish to talk with his workers. Little did I know that years later, I would be representing workers like these in their struggle for the right to unionize the fields.

Half a block past Salinas High School, I pulled into a driveway on Main Street marked with a small sign that read: "California Rural Legal Assistance." While I sat in the parking lot adjacent to the stucco office, generating enough courage to walk into my new office for the first time, a stocky Chicano[1] appeared.

"Are you the new lawyer?" he asked.

Offering his hand when I climbed from my VW bus, the young Mexican-American introduced himself. His name was Ladislao Piñeda.

"You a lawyer?" I asked while we walked across the parking lot toward the office entrance.

"A combination investigator and interpreter. They call me a community worker," he answered.

Piñeda stared at my long, bushy hair as he accompanied me into the small office. Like many legal service offices, it was adorned with an old wooden desk, a secondhand Naugahyde couch, and randomly placed metal folding chairs resting on a linoleum floor. On the corner coffee table sat an old lamp and pamphlets printed in English and Spanish: *How to Apply for Public Assistance*, *How to Handle Your Own Case in Small Claims Court*, and *You Too Can Live on a Budget*.

---

[1]Mexican American.

The tiny lawyers' offices each had an old wooden chair, a metal folding chair, a secondhand desk, and a bookshelf. The only set of books containing California codes or laws and the only set of books reporting the courts' interpretation of the codes were crammed into a nine-by-twelve storage room in the rear, which served as the library. Except for these codes and opinions that a retiring private attorney had donated and the legal texts CRLA lawyers purchased themselves, the only place we could find the law applicable to the varied legal problems that brought us clients was the county law library located on the second floor of the courthouse, half a mile away.

A year before I had even heard of California Rural Legal Assistance, a young lawyer by the name of Jim Lorenz with O'Melvany and Myers, the largest law firm in Los Angeles, convinced President Johnson's people in Washington D.C. to open nine law offices spread across rural California to represent farm workers. Lorenz recruited a Boston lawyer, Gary Bellow, to join him in the adventure. Meanwhile, Marty Glick, a slender, dark-haired *magna cum laude* Ohio State graduate who wanted to be a tax lawyer but was working for the Justice Department trying civil rights cases in the South, met Bob Gnaizda, who worked for the Internal Revenue Service. Glick and Gnaizda became friends and instead of Glick joining Gnaizda at the IRS doing tax law, Gnaizda agreed to join Glick in the South trying civil rights cases. Glick was working on a case the Justice Department filed against deputy sheriffs in Mississippi for the killing of civil rights activists Michael Schwerner, James Chaney, and Andrew Goodman, when he received a phone call at the Holiday Inn in McComb, Mississippi, from Gnaizda. Gnaizda had been recruited by Jim Lorenz. Instead of Gnaizda joining Glick in Mississippi, Gnaizda told Glick they were going to California to end the abuse and exploitation of farm workers. Glick and Gnaizda ended up in Salinas working for CRLA.

I already knew that my classmate Ralph Abascal was starting to work in the office. Since neither Abascal nor I had yet received bar exam results, the only licensed attorney in the office was Marty Glick.

In addition to the one lawyer, I met the one secretary, Amelia Harris; the receptionist, Angie Valenzuela; and a second community worker, José Pérez, who everyone called Joe. Amelia was a middle-age, middle-class, Mexican-American whose ancestors had settled the Salinas Valley when the Spanish arrived hundreds of years ago. She had married a Salinas fireman. Joe was a mild young guy whose goal was to get out of Salinas and move to San Francisco, but he, like the rest of the staff in the Salinas office of California Rural Legal Assistance, was determined to improve the lives of the less fortunate.

We later moved to a larger office nearer the courthouse, an older wooden house converted into an office large enough to provide space for our directing attorney, Denny Powell, who had transferred to Salinas from Madera; Bill Daniels, who had transferred from McFarland; Richard Gonzalez, a young attorney from New Mexico; Harvard graduate Dave Kirkpatrick; two community workers, Enrique Cantú and Manuel Olivas; our receptionist, Angie Valenzuela; three secretaries; and me. It was in the tiny storefront office on Main Street where I talked with thousands of farm workers and learned how to use the law to solve the problems they seemed to bring in nonstop.

Seven

THE FIRST CLIENT I SAW at CRLA was typical of the thousands I would see over the next seven years. Cristina Escobedo was from Calexico. She lived in Spreckles and supported herself and three kids on what she earned thinning lettuce in the spring and picking tomatoes all summer. She looked forty but was probably about twenty-five. A couple of years before I saw Mrs. Escobedo, she had bought a living-room set at a budget home furnishing store. The fast-talking salesman had convinced her she could easily pay the $3,300 at $49 a month. For two years she paid regularly. When one of her daughters was sick and Mrs. Escobedo had to pay for a doctor, she didn't pay her furniture bill. With two years of regular payments, Mrs. Escobedo assumed the seller would understand her missing one payment. She was wrong. Mrs. Escobedo showed me an envelope she had received. It was marked in red on the outside to tell the world: "YOU MUST OPEN THIS LETTER. YOU ARE BEING SUED FOR NONPAYMENT OF A LAWFUL DEBT." Inside the envelope was a form printed like a court order commanding her to pay the $3,312 principal and $400 in collection fees for a total of $3,712.

After Mrs. Escobedo left, I fruitlessly researched the law and, confused, finally asked Glick how she could make payments for two years and still owe more principal than she owed in the first place? Glick studied the papers Mrs. Escobedo brought to the office, grabbed a pencil, and scribbled on a legal pad. He explained, "She's paying 18 percent interest. $3,300 at 18 percent is $594 a year just in interest. Mrs. Escobedo has been paying $49 a month or $588 a year, six dollars less than the interest alone."

Every month for two years Mrs. Escobedo had paid $49 and owed more at the end of two years than when she started. She was paying more than a quarter of the money her family had to live on and if she continued to do so for the rest of her life, she'd always owe more and more.

I learned that morning a basic lesson about the life of a farm worker. No matter the workers color—brown, white, or black—it is a life, in many ways, not unlike the life of a medieval serf. It is a life that is not fair.

Each evening when I walked through the front door of the cottage I shared with Kathy and some raccoons, Kathy asked what I had done that day to help the poor. "I talked with a lot of clients," I usually responded. One evening I told her that during the afternoon, I had negotiated a deal to allow Mr. and Mrs. Campos to stay in their home instead of losing it in a foreclosure. On another I told her that I had stopped repossession of the González family's pickup. More than once I said that I had negotiated an agreement for a family to pay an unexpected medical bill over time rather than have the client's entire paycheck garnished by a greedy collection agency, leaving the family without food and with hungry children. Before I started working at CRLA, like most people, I thought legal assistance just helped the poor solve simple daily problems.

Apparently knowing that you don't win a war by just putting bandages on wounded warriors, the founders of CRLA had formed task forces on working conditions in the field, public benefits to disabled and elderly farm workers, farm worker housing, and the education of farm workers' children. Under the leadership of Gnaizda and Glick, the task force on working conditions helped to challenge misuse of the guest-worker or H-2 program that was stealing the jobs of California farm workers, and they fought to assure that for the first time farm workers had toilets and drinking water while they spent long hours working in California's hot fields.

In the Central Valley, the public-benefit task force with Sheldon Green, Phil Neumark, Fred Hiestand, and Daniel Lowenstein stopped Governor Ronald Reagan's proposal to deprive medical care and financial assistance to California's poor, most of whom were disabled, elderly, or blind. Under Ralph Abascal and Neil Levy's guidance, the task force prevented Reagan from obliterating California's assistance to poor children.

Led by Dave Kirkpatrick, the housing task force fought to prevent the closure of farm workers' housing during the cultivation season, developed new housing for farm workers in places like Calexico and Soledad, fought to stop discrimination against farm workers who wished to buy their own home, and prevented retaliatory eviction of farm workers who complained about unfit habitation.

The education task force, under the energy and enthusiasm of Marty Glick, gathered research and statistics, and brainstormed at monthly meetings of lawyers and community workers across the state on issues such as ensuring access to bilingual education for non-English-speaking students and challenging the placement of farm workers' children into dead-end curriculum tracks. When I arrived in Salinas, I joined the education task force. We gathered information on culturally-biased IQ testing and soon learned that far too many farm workers' children, like those of Chicanos and blacks across the state, were being labeled mentally retarded.

Working for CRLA meant a great deal more than helping farm workers solve the particular problems they brought through the door of our nine offices daily. Long hours spent at the office and in the fields were part of fighting the war on poverty, an epic campaign that involved efforts to challenge systematic inequalities in America.

Eight

ONCE A WEEK DURING THE EVENING, I drove to Soledad to see clients with a part-time community worker, Héctor de la Rosa. During the day, Héctor was a mechanic at the sole car dealer in town. Héctor was about twenty-five years old. He was born in Aguascalientes, Mexico. In the late 1940s when he was five, his father came to the United States as a bracero. After spending a season in Michigan, he returned, and Héctor's family emigrated without papers from Mexico to Atoka, New Mexico. Soon Héctor's father was employed on a farm. Héctor attended Atoka Elementary School for the next six years. A companion of Héctor's father traveled to California and returned with a car.

"You can get rich in California," he said. "Look, I was there a short time and I have a car already. Let's go."

It sounded good to Héctor's father, and there wasn't much of a future doing farm work in Atoka, New Mexico. He talked with Héctor's mother, and they were ready to go. Héctor's father told his employer he was leaving.

"No," his employer said. "You will starve in California. There are no jobs."

"No," we are leaving," Héctor's father replied.

That night, Héctor heard a knock. His father opened the door and there stood a tall Anglo in a green Border Patrol uniform. "Let me see your papers," he demanded.

"We have no papers," responded Héctor's father.

"Let's go," ordered the man Héctor described as "Smoky the Bear."

"We will do as you say," responded Héctor's father, "but my wife is going to give birth to a child any minute and you will be responsible for delivering the baby if it comes while we are on the way."

"I'll return in a month. Be ready to go," ordered the officer.

Exactly one month later, the Border Patrol officer returned.

For the following years, the De la Rosa family, now with a little brother for Héctor, lived in Torreón, Mexico. Apparently feeling guilty for having caused Héctor's family to be deported, the former employer filed an immigration application for the De la Rosas and even paid the fee himself. Four years after they had been deported, the De la Rosa family proceeded through the border inspection at Juárez and were migrant farm workers traveling to Texas to pick cotton, to New Mexico to pick beets, and to Arizona to pick tomatoes. In 1957 or 1958, the De la Rosas headed for San Jose, California, to pick prunes. Seeing green fields on all sides as he drove through Soledad, Héctor's father said, "We should stay here because there is life here." Needing the money they would earn in the San Jose harvest, they did not stop. When the season ended, the De la Rosas traveled to Oakland because a neighbor in Torreón had a son who lived in Oakland. As strangers, they knocked on the man's door. After their Oakland host unsuccessfully tried to find work for Héctor and his father, they left Héctor's mother and little brother in Oakland and headed south to look for work. They arrived in Salinas with 75 cents and little gas. They went to a farm labor camp on Sun Street, where they stood in line for dinner as if they lived there. The cook caught them, but apparently seeing their hunger gave them food.

When they asked if he knew where they could find work, the cook told them, "It is winter. There is no work now," but he allowed Héctor and his father to sleep in a small room behind the kitchen.

"It was cold," Héctor told me later. "But we didn't even have money for food, much less a motel. The worst was that we had no blankets."

The next morning, Héctor's father bought 75 cents worth of gas and they went to the Martin Camp, down the Salinas Valley near the O.P. Murphy fields, not far from Soledad.

Soledad was a small rural settlement that sat twenty-five miles south of Salinas. By the time I arrived in 1968, aside from the crumbling adobe mission built during the 1770s, Soledad's sole notoriety was its nearby prison confining about 10,000 of California's most violent inmates. In years to come, the population would include the likes of Charles Manson, who directed the murder of Hollywood star Sharon Tate; Sirhan

Sirhan, who assassinated Bobby Kennedy; and Juan Corona, a farm labor contractor who slashed the throats of more than twenty Northern California migrant workers. For the several thousand farm workers who lived in Soledad year round, it was a place to work stooped each summer in the lettuce, celery, or tomato fields, barely making enough to pay the rent and feed the children during the long rainy winter.

When Héctor and his father finally arrived at the Martin Labor Camp, they asked for work.

"We have braceros," the labor contractor told them. "We have no more work available."

Héctor's father pleaded. "We have no gas. We have no money. We have no food. We have nowhere else to go. Give us a bed and food, and that's all we ask for until we find another job."

"You can stay a week. Then you have to leave."

The next morning, Héctor held his first short-handled hoe. "I'll show you how to use it," the contractor said, "but complain and you're gone."

Héctor finished his first day stooped in the field. When he returned to the camp at dark, he was burning with fever. "Never again," he told his father. "I can't spend the day stooped in the field." Héctor was in too much pain to even eat supper that evening. "Pain shot across my back," he told me later. "I felt pain in places of my body that I didn't know existed."

The next morning, Héctor was back in the field with a short-handled hoe.

After three days, the Sunday before Christmas, the contractor gave them a few dollars to buy gas. They drove to Oakland, picked up Héctor's mother and brother, and that night Héctor and his father snuck the entire family into their room in the all-male labor camp.

The next day, Héctor's family went to look for a government camp a worker had told them about. The government camp was in Soledad. The camp manager, whom Héctor would come to know as *El Campero*, escorted them to a tiny room in a barrack that once held German prisoners of war. The barracks had been divided into separate living areas. As he opened the door to his new home, Héctor saw cockroaches scamper across the cold concrete floor from one barren cot to another. The camp had a common kitchen and just one restroom for men and just one other for women, neither with any stalls. Héctor later told me it hurt living there. At their home in Torreón, they had had a toilet inside, a bathtub, and their own kitchen. Now they had to trudge through the mud and rain from their room to the common restroom if they had to relieve themselves during the night.

From the Soledad labor camp, the De la Rosa family migrated. It was home base. Before long, Héctor was singing in the choir at the local Catholic church. One evening, the choir met at the home of a woman he knew as *La Abuela*.[1] There, Héctor saw a young girl who had just arrived from Mexico. La Abuela told him the young girl's name was María. Two years later, Héctor and María were married at the Catholic church. María accompanied Héctor on his migrant route to Idaho, Washington, and Oregon, for one year. When they returned, she told him, "No more." If Héctor continued to do farm work, he had to work around Soledad or go alone. Since there was no year-round farm work around Soledad, and Héctor could not stand to be away from María, he went to every business in Soledad looking for work. There weren't many businesses in the town of around 2,000 residents, including those who lived in the surrounding labor camps. Finally, the owner of the one car dealership in town, Joe Westcott, told Héctor, "We need someone to sweep out the garage and the showroom at night." Soon Héctor was an apprentice mechanic. Before long, their daughter Graciela was born, and Héctor, María, and Graciela moved to a one-bedroom cottage on the edge of town.

On my first night in Soledad in the fall of 1968, Héctor, María, and Graciela still lived in this same small wooden house facing the lettuce fields on the edge of town close to Soledad prison. María not only made the best enchiladas I ever tasted, but she taught my European taste buds about unconventional foods like chicken *mole*.[2]

Every Monday evening, Héctor and I saw clients in the Catholic church parish hall. Sometimes after seeing the clients, we went to Los Panchos Cantina to play pool.

---

[1] The Spanish term *La Abuela* means "the grandmother."
[2] *Mole* is a chocolate-based sauce that is prevalent in southern Mexican cuisine and is typically a complement to meat.

"Elmo, we don't have jobs, don't speak the language, don't have any money and we didn't ask the Mexican government for permission — is this legal?"

During the first half of the nineteenth century, Eastern settlers came west and took land that belonged to Mexico. In the twentieth century, the agribusiness industry that occupied and controlled the same land imported Mexicans who were held in bondage, without rights. (Courtesy of Dennis Renault, *The Sacramento Bee*)

Nine

NOT LONG AFTER I BEGAN WORKING IN SALINAS, Denny Powell and Bill Daniels arrived, José Pérez moved to San Francisco, and Ladislao Piñeda enrolled at the University of California, Santa Cruz. José and Ladislao were replaced by blond-haired Enrique Cantú and Manuel Olivas. Cantú was a former migrant farm worker from Mexico who considered Sanger, California, his home base. Cantú could hear a client tell of a problem and immediately saw the solution, but his Spanish accent was so strong, his English was barely understandable. We called him Henry (the English equivalent of "Enrique"). Olivas had been a Salinas homeboy who, although in his mid-20s, was still more likely to say *órale* than *está bien*, more likely to talk about his *jale* than his *trabajo*, and more likely to call his woman his *ruca* than his *novia*.[1]

One evening I was riding to Soledad with Cantú. On the way, we passed a "No Littering" sign. Henry laughed and told me that when he used to migrate from Chihuahua, Mexico to Texas to pick cotton, he saw "Litter Box" written on the side of huge trash containers. He could never understand why they were called little boxes. (Phonetically, the words "litter" and "little" might sound different to Northerners, but to Spanish speakers they sound the same.)

---

[1]The Spanish terms *órale* and *está bien* are, respectively, the slang and formal ways to say "cool" or "okay." The terms *jale* and *trabajo* mean job. *Ruca* and *novia* are Spanish terms for "girlfriend," the former being the informal use and the latter being the formal.

The next evening Cantú and I were in Soledad. After I finished talking with a woman having trouble getting food stamps because the welfare department didn't believe she had moved four times that year, I walked over to a table where Héctor and Henry talked with a young farm worker. After exchanging pleasantries, Hector urged the young laborer to tell me his story. It turned out, in fact, that the laborer was seeking help for a fellow migrant in need.

"This morning," began the dark young man, speaking slowly in perfect Spanish to help me comprehend, "I was irrigating the grapes where I work when a young woman called me over. She told me she needs to see a lawyer. She works for a labor contractor and stays at his camp."

"Where's the camp?" I asked.

"In the hills near Greenfield. Anyway, I told her about my friend Héctor and she asked me if he could come to the camp and talk with her."

"Why can't she come here?" I asked.

"She didn't say. All she said is the problem is very big, and she can't come to the office. She said Héctor should come to the camp Friday evening because that's the only time the contractor isn't there, and she wants to see Héctor when no one else is around. She seems very scared of something."

"Can you come to Soledad tomorrow night, boss?" Héctor asked me. "You and Henry can go see the woman. I have to go with John Saavedra to the credit union meeting." (At the time, Héctor and Saavedra were heavily involved in a CRLA-supported effort to help set up a credit union for farm workers in Soledad.)

After the worker who told us a woman wanted us to come by the labor camp left, I asked Héctor, "Wasn't the guy who let me use the short hoe a farm labor contractor? Is that the same thing as a contractor?"

Héctor grinned at my naiveté. The community worker, who quit school in the tenth grade to work in the fields (Héctor), then explained to the twenty-year schooled lawyer (me), "Farm labor contractors provide temporary workers to growers that don't want to hire their own workforce. Growers use them a lot on jobs that last only a few weeks like pruning, weeding, or harvesting."

"It sounds like they perform a valuable service."

"Sometimes, but too many are crooks. They don't care for the health and safety of the workers. They get an old bus somewhere with uncertain brakes or windshield wipers that could never be approved by the highway patrol to transport migrant laborers from one place to another to work the fields. It's totally unregulated. A couple years ago, about thirty farm workers were killed when a farm labor contractor drove across the railroad tracks in front of a train in Chular."

"Oh, shit," I responded, in shock.

Héctor sat silently.

Confused, I asked, "Dangerous driving makes them crooks?"

"Farm labor contractors get paid a set amount by the company to get a job done, like thinning 180 acres of lettuce or pruning 640 acres of grapevines. The less they pay the workers, the more profit for the farm labor contractors. They pay the workers very little and work them until they drop."

"You make labor contractors sound like hyenas or vultures cleaning the bones of the defenseless farm workers," I muttered. "Can't the workers just complain to the legal authorities?"

"What legal authorities, Mo? The police are too busy fighting real crime to care about farm labor contractors cheating farm workers. There's a state agency in Sacramento responsible for enforcing California's few labor laws, but I don't think it's ever heard of the Salinas Valley. Too often, when it comes to the farms and especially to farm labor contractors, there is no legal authority."

"That sucks," I commented.

"Yeah, especially since labor contractors can be very exploitative," continued Héctor. "Will you go to the camp with Henry?"

"If he's afraid to go alone. . . ." I began, thinking I might appeal to Henry's male pride in a way that would finally get me off the hook.

"It's not that I'm afraid . . ." Henry said, defensively.

"Is that a *macho* I hear?"[2] I asked, jokingly.

"No, man," Henry replied, "But it might not be that safe. I've heard of contractors killing people who get in their way. I can take care of myself, but I was just thinking. . . . You want to learn about farm workers, and if the woman has a hard legal problem, it'd be better if she talked to a lawyer. That's you, right?"

Henry's comment backed me into a corner that I knew now I could not get out of without accompanying him to the camp.

I felt my stomach churn.

---

[2] *Macho* is Spanish for "manly".

Ten

ON FRIDAY EVENING, the sun slipped behind the dark foothills between the Salinas Valley's lettuce and celery fields, and Big Sur's rugged coastline. In the twilight, Henry drove through the south edge of Soledad, past the ancient gas station with its fading green and white Quaker State sign, and weeds protruding from the cracked asphalt at the base of the two red and white pumps rusting at their edges. He drove past the mission, down the winding country road until turning onto an unmarked dirt trace. After a mile bouncing over potholes and lumps, we rounded a curve and ahead was silhouetted a weathered barn planted desolately on dark, damp earth; nearby was an outhouse. A water tap sprouted from the barrenness, a symbol of life and hope. The undershorts and socks scattered around the water hole, apparently laid out to dry, hinted of the land's inhabitants. I got out of Henry's Chevy when he parked the car and cautiously walked around.

"Looks like no one's here," I announced, sort of glad we might quickly be able to return to safer ground.

Suddenly, the outline of a woman's body appeared at the barn door, her face barely visible beneath the red bandana partially covering her black hair. Her eyes flicked frantically from side to side like a threatened gopher snake. Standing outside the haunting barn under the darkened sky, the woman spoke in a whisper.

"Can we go for a ride in your car?" she asked in Spanish. "There is too much danger here."

The woman sat in the rear seat riding through the unplanted lettuce fields while Henry drove away from the labor camp. In broken English, she began. "My name is Evangélica Ayala Santos. I was born twenty-four years ago. I had eighteen years when my father died." Evangélica told Henry and me that she heard how much money workers make in California. The United States had rejected her application for a visa since she had no money to guarantee her return home. She had considered taking the bus to Tijuana and finding a smuggler to help her cross the border, but her hopes had given way to her fear of rape and mayhem if caught by a ruthless border bandit or a deranged border patrol guard, so she had stayed in Mexico where it was safe.

Evangélica explained that on a bright September afternoon several months before in the village of her birth, she and her boyfriend Juan stood to be married in their pueblo's plaza. After the wedding, their families and friends danced and drank and shouted their ancestors' cries.

"I have much to say and not much time," Evangélica said. "The fat man will return to the camp before ten."

Henry glanced at his watch; his eyes reflected concern.

Speaking rapidly, Evangélica told us that during the wedding, two men pulled into town in a long blue Cadillac. They parked at the plaza and got out of the big car. "They looked funny in their wrinkled colored shirts and sunglasses walking among us dressed-up *mexicanos* enjoying ourselves," Evangélica said. "Finally, one of the strangers, the fat one, talked to my cousin and his friend, who were sitting on a bench watching all the pretty young *señoritas* walk by."

"The one you call the fat one," asked Henry, "is that the labor contractor?"

"*Sí, señor*. He asked my cousins if they knew anyone who wanted work." The stranger told Evangélica's cousin that he was from California and worked for a large agricultural company that needed workers. He said the pay was good and he would take them to the United States and provide a place to live and food.

"Sounds familiar," said Henry. He shook his head slowly, holding back the anger escaping from his azure eyes.

Within forty-eight hours of Evangélica's wedding, sixteen residents of her village were on a bus to the border. She told us that when the bus stopped at a small *plaza* in Mexicali around noon the day after leaving the mountain village, the contractor posted guards to keep Evangélica and her neighbors from leaving. At midnight a *coyote* drove them,[1] eight at a time, several kilometers from town and left them in the black desert. He told the frightened group to follow the trail until they came to a highway. Someone would be there to meet

---

[1] The Spanish term *coyote* in this context means "labor smuggler" or "illegal trafficker."

them. If they saw the *migra* (INS agents), they were to scatter and run.
"You made it across the border," I said.

"*Sí*. And hid in the bushes near the highway, shivering."

Just before dawn, the contractor drove up in a lettuce truck. He
ordered the now illegal immigrants to crowd into the enclosed rear.
The next day they arrived at the Greenfield labor camp. Scrambling
from the hot truck they gasped for fresh air.

Evangélica stopped talking when a pickup truck the color of Border Patrol vehicles pulled into an A & W lot close to where we were
parked. She smiled with relief when two women in short blouses and
cut-off jeans disembarked from the vehicle.

Evangélica continued. "I told Juan we should not have come. It
was very hot. We had not eaten since the journey, and I was too
embarrassed to pee in the back of that truck with all the men looking."
Evangélica told us she did not want to be here. She wanted to go
home.

Juan told her it would be better after they started working the next
morning. When the season was over they would have enough money
to return home and buy a cow. Their babies would always have food
and never have to come to this rich but dangerous land.

"He was wrong," said Henry.

"*Sí*. Now I am here alone and they have put Juan in jail. I cannot
go home."

"What do you mean you can't go home?" asked Henry.

"The *contratista* will not let me.[2] I am his slave."

"What do you mean?" I asked.

Evangélica told us that after she and Juan had arrived from Mexico, the fat man told them they owed $500 for the mule who carried
them here and $500 for the *coyote* who brought them across the bor-
der. Evangélica said she didn't think it was fair because no one told
them about these charges when they were luring them from their village. It was so much, but what could they do?

Evangélica told us they earned a dollar an hour, which was more
than farm workers earned in Mexico, but she soon learned things cost
much more here. The farm labor contractor charged them five dollars
a night for their cot, two dollars for dinner, a dollar for breakfast, a

---

[2]*Contratista* is Spanish for "labor contractor."

dollar for lunch, and a dollar each day for wine he bought for workers. Evangélica told us she did not drink wine.

"Did you tell him that you don't drink?" Henry asked.

Evangélica nodded. "He say I have to pay even if I don't drink the wine. Since we work so many hours a day, usually eleven or twelve, we earn enough to pay for our bed and food and even the wine, but he also charges us three dollars for interest each day on the $1,000 he says we owe for the trip here."

"That comes to $13 each day," Henry said.

"Each day we owe one dollar more than we earn. The *pendejo* will not let us leave until we pay what we owe."[3]

"You said now you are alone, your husband is in jail?" Henry asked.

"The *migra* came to the field. I hid in the vines so they did not see me, but now I wish they did catch me."

Believing Evangélica had finished her tale, I sat wondering to myself, *What can I do?*

Evangélica continued. After the *migra* took her husband away, the *contratista* came to her in the field. He wanted to see Evangélica after work. "I was happy. I thought he was going to help free Juan and let us go back to Mexico. When he came that night in his big car, all he wanted was to make sure I would continue working until I paid what he said I owed him. He told me that if I try to leave without paying what Juan and I owe, he will catch me and take me to a bar in Chular, called La Fiesta, where I will have to do it with all the foul *cabrones* in heat who line up and pay the money. The contractor says I will pay my debt by letting all the men put their thing in me."

I cursed. "I'm sorry, Evangélica. We have to tell the police. They'll arrest him. You'll be free."

"I cannot," Evangélica sobbed. "He will kill me."

"But if we go to the police now, they'll arrest him and you can leave. He can't bother you if he's in jail."

"I am sorry, *abogado*, but I do not trust the police as much as you.

---

[3]*Pendejo* is Spanish for "idiot" or "stupid."

I must be back in the camp before he returns."

While Henry was driving Evangélica back to the barn, she asked if he would take her to the bus station in Salinas instead. When he agreed, she asked if he could loan her money for a ticket. Henry dropped Evangélica off at the Greyhound station, placing several crumpled bills in her hand to cover her fare back to Mexico.

On the ride from the bus station to my VW bus, I sat with confused feelings. "I know Evangélica's life will be better," I said.

Henry remained silent.

"I hate this job sometimes," I complained, searching for a scapegoat. "There are so many people in the fields struggling for survival. We don't even have time to fight poverty. We spend all our time representing people who bring their crises into the office, and we help so few. What about the war on poverty?"

"You have to find a way to win suits affecting thousands of people or hundreds of thousands at one time," suggested Henry. "We aren't going to win this war by worrying about mosquitoes while torn bodies lay all over the battlefield."

Eleven

ONE MONDAY EVENING, I went to Soledad with Ralph Abascal and Cantú when gray-haired Guadalupe and his wife Lupe Serna came into the CRLA office. *"¿En qué les puedo servir?"* inquired Ralph, asking how he might help the farm worker couple.

I listened carefully, still not secure with my Spanish, to a tale that led Ralph and me into our first legal adventure involving the schools. *"Señores abogados*, you know our son Francisco."

"Sure, the miler at Gonzalez High," replied Ralph.

"Yes," continued Guadalupe. "He is a good student as well as a fast runner. Francisco is a senior now."

"Really. I know they love him in Gonzalez."

"They love Francisco when he wins the mile race every Friday at the track contest. But Señora Álvarez, the teacher, is the only one who cares he is also a good student. She has talked with Francisco about going to college." Paula Álvarez taught at Gonzalez High School attended by the students living in Soledad and the rest of the central Salinas Valley.

"Good," Ralph smiled.

"The school principal does not think so. He laughs at Francisco for having such a dream."

Lupe and Guadalupe Serna and their ten children lived in an old farmhouse just south of Gonzalez. "Francisco, he is the seventh," explained Lupe. "All his older brothers and sisters did good in school. They stayed out of trouble. But none thought about going to college. They all work in the fields. We have enough from what all of us earn to pay for Francisco to go to college. Señora Álvarez says they have loans and maybe he will get money from the school if he studies real

50

hard. We are proud to be farm workers, but with an education, Francisco will not be out of work in the winter. He can buy a nice house and a car, and have money for his own children to someday go to college."

"*Perdón, señora,*" interrupted Abascal, "I have great respect for your family. What Francisco does is important not just for Francisco but as an example for all the kids in Soledad. But why do you need our assistance?"

"Perhaps you will speak with Mrs. Álvarez?"

Abascal and Manuel Olivas agreed to go to Gonzalez to see the young teacher. Cantú and I were in Soledad.

Abascal and Olivas later told me that they had gone to see the teacher, Paula Álvarez, in Gonzalez after school hours to consult with her about our conversation with the Sernas. When they got to her home, they saw Francisco, the aspiring student and track star, waiting out front on the sidewalk and called him over as they pulled the car to a stop. Francisco walked up to the car window.

"Francisco," said Abascal, rolling his window down. "We didn't expect you to be in Gonzalez so late."

"We, some of the other students who like Mrs. Álvarez, and I, heard you were coming by," the young man reported. "We stayed around to tell you how much we want you to help her."

"Be honest with me, Francisco," Abascal requested. "Is Mrs. Álvarez afraid to see us alone? Me being a lawyer?"

"Naw, man. You're paranoid. We just got her into this mess and we want to help her. All of us feel real bad."

"Well, let's go talk with her. You know we'll do what we can," said Abascal as he and Héctor got out of the car to approach the teacher's home.

"She's not here, sirs," said Francisco. "Her apartment is real small and so many of us want to help her, we're meeting at the high school. Come on, I'll show you where her classroom is."

Ten minutes later, Abascal, Héctor, and Francisco entered a class-room at the school. A number of Mexican-American students surrounded the teacher, who was a young woman in her early twenties.

"You're Paula Álvarez, I presume," grinned Abascal, his hand outstretched as he walked toward the petite raven-haired teacher. "I'm Ralph Abascal. This is Manuel Olivas."

"I know Manuel, Mr. Abascal," laughed Mrs. Álvarez. "And Francisco has told me all about you."

Héctor then encouraged the teacher to talk about why the Sernas, their son Francisco, and the other students were rallying to support her. "Paula, Francisco's parents have spoken very highly of you to Ralph. Why don't you tell us what the problem is."

"I don't know exactly where to start," began the teacher. "I came to the school last fall full of hope. Ten years ago, I was a high school student myself. Now, I'm the first Mexican-American teacher in Gonzalez High School's history. The fall went all right. I kept quiet and smiled a lot. Then this spring the students started a MECHA chapter. You know what that is, the Mexican American Chicano Association. They asked me to be their advisor, and I gladly accepted the honor. Soon, I was encouraging the MECHA members to continue their education after graduation, to go to college . . . students who had never given it a thought. This year, for the first time in history, many Chicanos took the SAT."

"The Scholastic Aptitude Test?" inquired Abascal.

"Uh huh. I think in the old days when you went to school it used to be called the College Entrance Exam. Anyway, where was I? Oh, yeah. Every MECHA member who took the test has been accepted by either a four-year college, like San Jose State, or a community college, like Hartnell in Salinas. One even got a scholarship to Berkeley. She. . . ." The teacher paused, extending her arm toward a tiny teenager, "will be the Salinas Valley's first Chicana doctor."

The dark youth blushed.

"Anyway," continued Mrs. Álvarez, appearing more at ease, "in April, the principal came to my room after school and said he wanted to talk with me. Before I knew what was going on, I was hearing, 'You're ruining the self-image of the Mexican-American students.

You know they'll start college in September and flunk out by Christmas. Don't you know they want to work in the fields so they can get new cars? But you're pressuring them to go to college. You're making it a *macho* thing.'

"I couldn't believe it. That white s.o.b. telling me about the self-image of Mexican-Americans, as if he even cared. It's funny. I thought he was kind of a nice guy. I knew he tried hard but had no backbone. He will do anything the growers who run the school district want. He's joined with them to come down on me because I sponsor MECHA and want its members to further their education. Plus, they know we help César Chávez on the grape boycott."

Abascal nodded slowly.

Paula continued. "The growers don't want the Mexicans going to college because they think their place is in the fields. Anyway, I'd heard enough. I told the principal to get out of my classroom. Well that did it. Since then, everything I do is wrong. I get pink slip after pink slip. A couple days ago, I got notice they will not be needing me next year."

"Are they eliminating your position?" Abascal gently asked the angry young teacher.

"No. It's all crap. They'll hire someone to replace me before this year's over. But what can I do?"

"Well, *jefe*,"[1] said Olivas, looking at Abascal, "what do you think?"

Abascal sat silently for a moment. As if thinking aloud he began, "There are several ways we can approach it. You don't have a union, so filing a grievance is out. I don't think the district can legally fire you for encouraging students to go to college, but I'm learning that what the law says doesn't make much difference in the local courts. Maybe with the students protesting, a civil rights suit in federal court will cause the district to back down."

Three weeks later, instead of going to their classes, students went eighty miles north to San Jose to support their teacher in the federal court. They cheered when the school board's attorney apologetically told Judge Robert Peckham, "The district board has reconsidered the

---

[1]*Jefe* is Spanish for boss.

needs for the fall semester and will retain Mrs. Álvarez on the faculty."

As they walked from the courthouse, the school district's attorney explained to Abascal, "It was all a misunderstanding."

Through its last-minute reconsideration, the Gonzalez School District avoided having Paula Álvarez's Mexican-American students tell Judge Peckham, with television cameras rolling and newspaper reporters scribbling, that they were going to college because Mrs. Álvarez convinced them they could better their own and their families' lives by following the American Dream of furthering their education.

Twelve

In 1965, Marty Glick, Bob Gnaizda, and Ladislao Piñeda opened a Salinas office to commence the work of California Rural Legal Assistance. After Abascal and I arrived in Salinas, Glick and Gnaizda moved to San Francisco, where Gnaizda opened Public Advocates, an organization of young public interest lawyers who fought the war on poverty as a private law firm: and Glick became CRLA's director of litigation.

Not long after I started working at California Rural Legal Assistance, I went with Glick and an ivy-league attorney, Peter Coppleman, a hundred miles south of Salinas to Atascadero. The Atascadero School District had stopped bussing to school the children who lived in the country surrounding the small town. Many of the children, who had no other way to get to school, lived in grower-provided housing with their farm worker parents. While in Atascadero, since both Marty and Peter wore goatees and were easily identified as outsiders, we felt the paranoia of being watched and followed by the town's conservative leadership most of the time we were there. One evening while we talked about the growing distrust and loathing CRLA staff was feeling throughout much of rural California, I complained to Marty that I was more bothered by the high number of clients who came into our offices needing legal assistance. He told me that soon after he started at Rural Legal Assistance he realized that, if we were going to fight the multitude of problems our clients faced with our very limited number of attorneys, we had to use class action lawsuits whenever possible. In a class action, the plaintiffs sue for themselves and all others similarly situated. Marty believed class actions were a way to really fight the war on poverty. He wanted us to focus on solving problems in singular lawsuits rather than filing thousands of individual suits to remedy what was essentially the same wrong. He warned me that we couldn't use a class action to stop all repossessions of farm workers' cars or to stop all evictions of farm worker families from their homes; since these cases usually did not involve common factual situations, but he recommended that whenever I had the chance, I try to seek relief not only for my client but also for all persons similarly situated.

"Can I file a class action to stop stoop labor?" I asked half-seriously.

Glick chuckled. "I think you need more than a class action to stop stoop labor."

Soon, Marty, Héctor, and I would try to seek relief in a class action.

It began one cold Monday night in Soledad. Héctor and I walked through the brisk wind from the Catholic church parish hall where we saw clients. As we made our way to the parking lot, a farm worker approached us.

I recognized him immediately. His name was Carlos Molina. "Do you have a moment to speak?" Molina whispered to us in Spanish. Over the previous couple of years, I had represented Molina to help him address six or eight minor problems.

"Sure, with a friend," I replied, shaking his small, callused hand.

"Would you do me the favor of coming to our home?" asked the five-foot-tall farm worker, his deeply creased brown face looking far older than his years. "It will be more private."

"Can we talk here?" I asked, looking at my watch. "I still have to drive clear to Aptos."

"I understand, lawyer. If you don't have time, I will wait. But it is a private matter. It is about my son Ramón."

We agreed that we would talk later, and Hector and I proceeded to make our way to Aptos to deal with another matter awaiting us there.

Molina lived with his chubby wife and many children in a city-run labor camp on the east edge of town. It was the same camp that Héctor had made home shortly after arriving in Soledad ten years earlier. Although the camp units had electricity, the power was often out.

I initially represented Molina in an effort to restore the electricity. Within a few months, I again represented his family when the camp manager threatened them with eviction for complaining about the overflowing septic tank, and again after Molina complained of rent that seemed to increase almost monthly. Looking across the lettuce field from the camp, the residents could not avoid seeing the sixteen-foot chain-link fence crowned with flesh-cutting razor wire that enclosed Soledad prison.

Walking to Molina's door from Héctor's Plymouth station wagon, some days after he approached us in the church parking lot, I saw the surrounding farm workers' homes rising from harsh gray dirt, boxes covered with chipped and faded gray-green paint with a decaying door every twenty feet. A prisoner-of-war camp atmosphere prevailed. The drab gray-green boxes were lined up in the barren landscape. Not a blade of grass choked its way through the parched earth. The Molina's home, like most of the others, had a cracked and broken front door. I knocked on the wall adjacent to the torn screen. Molina answered.

Over a small wooden table hung a single lightbulb. The cement floor was nearly covered with veteran army cots. An ancient stove sat in one corner, a small refrigerator in another. There was a tiny sink and a tinier kitchen counter. An inviting aroma forced us to sample beans and homemade tortillas.

Speaking very slowly in Spanish, Señor Molina began telling me about his latest problem. While Héctor, Molina, and I ate, the farm worker's wife stood before the old black-metal stove warming more tortillas. Winter wind crept through broken windows and slivered through the gap below the door. Except for an open oven, there was no internal heating.

Handing me the steaming pot of pinto beans, Molina told us, "Ramón has nine years. He should be in the fourth grade, but the school decided he cannot learn. The school placed Ramón in a class with eight other children. They call it the mental retard class. All the children in the class are from farm worker families." Thus, Molina began a tale that kept Héctor and me at his kitchen table until after two the next morning.

Héctor confirmed that all the children in the class were *mexicanos.*

"*Sí.* I know my son, and I know the other children. They might not be too smart but they are not mental retards."

I felt my stomach tighten. *Not only does the agribusiness industry consider the farm workers who provide our food an inferior underclass,* I thought, *but even our schools throw the children of farm workers into the same inferior caste.*

"I don't know Ramón well," I told Molina. I had seen the youth several times at my office when he interpreted for his father. I had seen him play Little League baseball with his friends. He seemed normal, but I was no expert on mental retardation.

Molina called his son Ramón over to the table so we could speak with him. The Spanish-speaking nine-year-old told me he was tested in English.

"Ramón, your mom and dad don't speak English, do they?"

"*No, señor.*"

"You speak English and Spanish?" I asked.

"*Sí, señor.* We speak only Spanish at home. Me and my friends, we speak only in Spanish when we are playing, but at school they don't let us speak Spanish. Some of my classmates cannot talk in school the whole day because they do not speak English."

"Did the people giving the test for the special class ask whether you wanted to be tested in English or Spanish?"

"*No, señor.* They just tell me to answer the questions. I don't even know what the test is for."

"What about the other kids in your class, were they tested in Spanish?"

"I don't think so."

"Do they all speak both English and Spanish?"

"Besides me, four do."

"And all the others speak English?"

"*No, señor.* They speak only Spanish."

Near two, while we were saying good evening, Molina walked Héctor and me to our car.

"Thank you for coming to my home," Molina said. My wife said a lawyer would not come to our home, especially a *güero* lawyer."

I stared silently into the farm worker's dark eyes.

"As you know, we don't have money for lawyers," he continued. "So the companies and the schools do whatever they want with us and our children. No one can stop them."

"It's getting better," I said. "A few years ago, there was no one. At least now, there's Rural Legal Assistance and the farm workers' union."

Molina shook his head slowly. "César's just starting," he said. "His union is our dream. You and Héctor have helped me, but we are afraid the government will take away your money because CRLA helps the poor too much. I hope before it does, you will stop the schools from calling our children retards."

Thirteen

WITH MOLINA'S WORDS, Héctor, Glick, and I hustled to make our way through the topsy-turvy maze of intelligence testing. When Héctor and I told Marty we had found the case we so desperately wanted to bring, he was as excited as we were. Within days, Marty, Héctor, and I met with all nine children in the Soledad Elementary School class for the mentally retarded. Although they didn't appear mentally retarded, we knew we were not competent to make that determination. Marty would vividly remember Arturo reciting to him the uniform numbers and statistics of San Francisco 49er football players. Diana was shy, as were most of the nine children. All spoke almost no English. All came from homes where only Spanish was spoken. All were tested in English.

Marty and I left the meeting with the nine children wanting to do two things that potentially conflicted. We wanted to get Ramón and the other eight children out of the mentally retarded class and into a transition program as soon as possible. At the same time, we didn't want to lose the opportunity to have the nine children represent a class of similarly situated children who could sue to stop the racially discriminatory placement of tens of thousands of Spanish-speaking children in classes for the mentally retarded across the state.

The next morning I called a professor, Steve Valdez, who taught psychology at San Diego State University. Over Memorial Day weekend, I drove five hundred miles south to talk with Dr. Valdez.

"Let me look into it," responded Professor Valdez after learning about the problem. "If necessary, I'll fly up to Soledad and evaluate the children."

On the Fourth of July, I picked Dr. Valdez up at the San Jose airport. During the eighty-mile ride south on Highway 101 to Soledad, through the garlic fields and cherry orchards surrounding Gilroy, and the Prunedale apple orchards, the psychologist told me that even though he grew up speaking Spanish, he couldn't accurately measure the intelligence of children who grow up in a farm labor camp speaking Spanish. "It's like trying to determine the intelligence of African-American youths that grow up on the streets of South Central Los Angeles," he said. He explained some kids on Los Angeles streets show genius through contact with friends and authorities in their daily life, but an intelligence test score says they're retarded. "We don't even have a test to determine the intelligence of nonmainstream children. We're forced to use a standard intelligence test, but at least we can administer it in a language the children understand."

Passing Salinas Valley lettuce fields, the doctor explained that labeling a child mentally retarded can lead to the child fulfilling that expectation. "Tell a little girl she's mentally retarded," explained Dr. Valdez, "and treat her as retarded, and low and behold, you'll develop a mentally retarded young lady. Had the same girl been told from birth she was gifted and been treated as gifted, she could attend Stanford."

Dr. Valdez tested in Spanish all the Soledad children in the class for the mentally retarded. Eight of the nine children scored in the normal range. Before leaving Soledad, the doctor showed me some of the incorrect answers the Soledad children had given. Most had incorrectly answered such questions as "Why is it better to pay bills by check than cash?" and "What color is a ruby?"

"Steve. How do questions like these show intelligence?" I asked in dismay. "Don't they just tell the tester the child doesn't know what he or she hasn't been exposed to?"

With his head shaking sadly and sarcasm in his tone, Dr. Valdez told me that as a layman I might think so, but to experts, wrong answers on too many questions show us a child has an IQ below 70 and is therefore mentally retarded. Too many school psychologists believe their job is to tattoo on each child an IQ number, like the SS placed on incarcerated Jews in Auschwitz.

Within days, Glick and I met with the Monterey County psychologist who tested the children. Glick's recollection is that Cruz

Reynoso, now the director of Rural Legal Assistance, may have come down to Salinas from his San Francisco office to join us. We learned that the school placed the farm workers' children in the mentally retarded class after they scored below 70 on a standard intelligence test. When he asked the psychologist about the children's language difference, Marty would clearly recall years later that the testing expert admitted, "I wondered about testing those children in English, but that was all we had." We urged the district to immediately remove the nine children from the mentally retarded class and provide them with transition education and support services. The county educators with whom we met appeared to agree. They said they would get back to us.

We left the meeting knowing that we were helping our clients but providing no help to the tens of thousands of Latino children across the state who had been erroneously labeled mentally retarded because their primary language was not English.

To the best of our recollection, a week or two later at the Soledad Elementary School District board meeting, with Glick and me glaring from the front row of the crowd of farm workers whose children had been labeled mentally retarded, the one-school district's superintendent told us in an angry and defensive manner that he was not removing Ramón and his classmates from the class for the mentally retarded. He was not the one who determined the children were retarded. The specialists did. All he did was place children in the class for the mentally retarded when the specialists told him they scored below an acceptable level on the IQ test. He believed that the specialists had followed the rules and done the right thing, but he would look into the matter further if it would satisfy us.

"Does the district receive additional money from the state for each child identified as mentally retarded?" Glick asked when the board opened the meeting to questions from the audience.

"Of course," responded the superintendent.

"So it is in the district's financial interest to identify slow learners or other hard-to-teach children as mentally retarded?"

"Are you trying to say we place children in the class for the mentally retarded to get money from the state?" the superintendent replied.

Glick smiled. *No further questions*, I thought silently. Marty and

I decided to sue immediately. Our clients should not be forced to spend another year in the mentally retarded class while bureaucrats studied the matter.

In addition to learning that the school had mislabeled our nine Soledad clients, Glick and I learned that each year California school districts placed hundreds of thousands of children in special classes for the mentally retarded. They relied on a respected intelligence test. Thirteen percent of the millions of children attending school in California were Spanish-surnamed, but 27 percent of the children in classes for the mentally retarded were Spanish-surnamed. A grossly disproportionate share of these students came from rural farm worker homes. It was time for a class action suit to stop the wholesale mislabeling of farm workers' children across the state as mentally retarded. We filed *Diana v. Board of Education* in San Francisco federal court before one of the fairest and brightest lights in modern American judicial history, Judge Robert Peckham. We told in legal papers the story we had learned in Soledad, Salinas, and Sacramento. We sought relief for the nine Soledad children and all children in the state similarly situated.

The State brought in one of its most experienced lawyers to oppose Glick and me. Sitting with Glick at counsel table, Glick looked confident. I felt a nervous chill run down my arms. The smooth-talking State lawyer told the patient federal judge that we had cost a small school district thousands of dollars defending itself in a frivolous lawsuit. When I heard the deep-voiced lawyer remind the judge that Glick and I had no training or experience in the area of mental retardation, did not understand the children's special needs, and had no right to come into court and scream racism, holding ourselves out as experts in intelligence testing, I knew I was in over my head. I prayed my inexperience in court would not prevent me from saying the right words to convince Judge Peckham that it was wrong to label children mentally retarded and throw them into the coral reef of low expectations merely because they obtained low scores on a test of their intelligence administered in a language they did not understand. Fortunately, Marty argued the case superbly in his simple clear manner. He knew he would have to defeat a controversial but "authoritative" study of scholars who had recently concluded that Latino and Black children score lower on intelligence than their white counterparts because they are inherently inferior. Glick had read and re-read Leon Kamin's work on inconsistencies that can result with proper manipulation, even when testing the intelligence of separated twins. He had consulted extensively with Kamin and persuasively explained to the court the bias of standardized intelligence tests, even when a child is tested in her primary language. He convinced Judge Peckham that testing a Spanish-speaking child in English is outrageous. He had done his homework diligently. He knew he was better prepared than the State lawyer.

The black-robed federal judge listened to the argument, took the matter under submission, recessed for a short time, and returned to the bench. He advised the attorney who represented the State Board of Education that it might be in his client's best interest to find a way to settle the matter. The State's attorney took the hint and we began negotiating. Marty and I left San Jose with a court order prohibiting school personnel from labeling a child mentally retarded because of the score received on an IQ test administered in a language other than the child's primary language, and requiring the State to retest on a culture-fair basis around 100,000 California-school children placed in classes for the mentally retarded as a result of a score achieved on a test administered in a language other than their primary language. After reevaluation, it was determined that around 55,000 California children had been erroneously labeled mentally retarded because their families had come from Mexico and the children had not yet become fluent in English.

It wouldn't have happened without nine brave little Soledad children, or without Marty Glick, or without an honest psychologist from San Diego. California can never again place Spanish-speaking children in classes for the mentally retarded because they score low on a standard intelligence test administered in a language they barely comprehend.

Fourteen

SEVERAL MONTHS AFTER the federal court order in *Diana v. Board of Education*, I met the Ojeda family. The Ojeda children attended elementary school. Each year their parents paid property taxes for teacher salaries and books. During the day, Mrs. Ojeda helped her children's teachers instruct Spanish-speaking kindergarten children. Señor Ojeda was active with the PTA in the evenings. Mr. and Mrs. Ojeda wanted to vote for school board members who determined what and how their children were taught. Although the Ojeda family had been permanent U.S. residents for nearly twenty years, they were not citizens. They could not vote.

A summer law student in our office, Luis Jaramillo, and I prepared a writ of mandate for the California Supreme Court on behalf of the Ojeda family and all others similarly situated. We pointed out to the court that on May 7, 1879, California adopted a citizenship requirement for voters. The same day, it prohibited Chinese- and African-Americans from owning land in the state. I knew that cases that should be sure winners are often lost. But my belief in why the Ojeda's should prevail grew when I read a letter to the editor a few days later in the Salinas newspaper, *The Californian*. The letter, submitted by a responsible local citizen, read in part:

> As [the nation commemorates the coming bi-centennial of] the Boston Tea Party, we are reminded that the abuse protested at the time was that of taxation without representation. Mr. Ojeda and others who brought this suit are attempting to remedy through nonviolent, legal means the same abuse that the early colonists confronted. As permanent resident aliens, these people have paid property taxes, income taxes, sales taxes and all the

other taxes to which we are all subject. Because their children are directly affected in school by determinations of the school board and its administrators, they have a real interest in who sits on that board. And yet they are denied the right to vote.

Several weeks later without stating a reason, the high court denied our petition for the writ. Sitting in my Salinas office, I stared at the court's order and an editorial in the Salinas *Californian* calling our lawsuit frivolous. I began to understand this was the consequence ordinary people face whenever they try to change a deeply rooted inequity, no matter how illogical. I was learning that logic and reason, and what is right, don't always prevail in the courts.

Fifteen

THE FOLLOWING SPRING I taught a poverty law class at the University of California at Santa Cruz. One evening I was driving down from San Francisco to teach my course when standstill traffic halted my ride over the hill from San Jose. I turned on the radio and anxiously switched from station to station, from rock and roll to mariachis to Willie Nelson, searching for a traffic report. My frustration turned to a grin when I heard the radio broadcaster say that Highway 17 was again open. Law enforcement had cleared the link between Santa Cruz and the Bay Area of 20,000 students who had blocked the road when they joined hundreds of thousands across the nation to protest Nixon's Cambodia invasion. Police had arrested scores of local students.

I was barely out of the driver's seat at the university when Ladislao Piñeda and Francisco Serna briskly walked to my car. A year after I had started working in Salinas, Piñeda left Rural Legal Assistance and began attending the university as a full-time student. Several years earlier, while at Gonzalez High School, Serna had convinced us to stop the school from firing his history teacher, Paula Álvarez, because she encouraged farm workers' children to attend college. Both were now students in my class at the university.

"Were you involved in the demonstration?" I asked.

"*Simón,*" replied Serna. "Almost everyone on campus was. They arrested me. Will you be my lawyer?"

"I heard they arrested about forty students."

"Yeah," replied Francisco. "It's the same old shit. They busted twenty-two minority students who weren't doin' nothing but taking part in the demonstration."

"But they arrested White students, too, didn't they?"

"The only *güeros* busted were the few who had loudspeakers," Ladislao responded. "To think I was dumb enough to believe I could get away from cop racism when I left the fields."

Three other arrested students were in my class, Carol Loo, Darnell Washington, and Alma Spring Water. At the class's request, I agreed to represent all twenty-two minority students arrested in the demonstration.

On the day of the arrests, sheriff's deputies booked the demonstrators but released them on their promise to appear at the arraignment a week later. At the arraignment, the court advised the students they were charged with obstructing the roadway and failing to disperse when ordered to do so by a law enforcement officer. The judge explained the defendants' constitutional right to a jury trial, to confront and cross-examine witnesses against them, and to remain silent. Each of the twenty-two students I represented entered a not guilty plea and requested a jury trial. The court consolidated the cases for one trial.

As the trial approached, one night after work I drove onto the University of California campus among the redwood-covered hills just north of Santa Cruz. Leaving downtown Santa Cruz, I passed one-hundred-year-old Victorian homes and maneuvered the curving single-lane road gradually rising across open fields to the campus buildings that sat among the redwoods like natural growth. In a Merrill College classroom I met with the twenty-two student demonstrators. Native-American Alma Spring Water reminded me that the thousands of Santa Cruz students who blocked the highway were following an American tradition stretching back to and beyond Sam Adams and the Sons of Liberty in exercising the power of people. The twenty-two student demonstrators wanted to show they were in the road protesting the United States' unlawful invasion of Cambodia.

I told them it was their right to tell the world from the witness stand why they had blocked the highway. "You may believe your conduct was morally right," I warned them, "but as a legal defense to the criminal charges, I don't think what you believe is going to keep you out of jail." I told them the district attorney was offering them a deal; plead guilty to one charge, he would dismiss the other charge, and they would have to serve no jail time.

"What about us being the victims of racial discrimination by the police?" asked Francisco. The only students arrested were a handful of Anglos and many more of the African-Americans, Chicanos, Asians, and Native-Americans in the street.

"That's your second defense," I responded to Francisco. "It has legal merit, but most jurors in this county are elderly, conservative, and white." I knew that it was unlikely I could convince a Santa Cruz jury that the police would discriminate against dark-complected students in favor of long-haired men and braless women who were white.

"So probably neither defense will get us off," said Chinese-American Carol Loo.

"The DA's offering probation with no jail time if you plead guilty," I reminded them.

"I'm for it," African-American Darnell Washington exclaimed. "I got enough going against me without a criminal record. I accept the offer."

"Well, I'm standing behind what I believe in," said Loo. "I don't care if I lose the trial."

"The DA said all of you have to accept the offer or it's off," I counseled. "It's a package deal."

"Same old divide-and-conquer shit the white man's been doing for centuries," lamented Sweet Water.

When most of the charged students sided with Loo, Washington yielded and the group unanimously rejected the offer.

"I'm not sure your decision is the most rational to keep you out of jail," I said, "but I respect you for standing behind what you believe in. We need to go over testimony. . . ."

"Can't that wait, Mr. Jourdane?" asked Loo. "Can you tell us a little about what will happen at trial?"

"Sure, if you want." I told the defendants that to convict them, a jury had to unanimously agree the prosecution proved beyond a reasonable doubt that they committed the crime and had no legal defense. If they got one juror to accept their side and hold firm while the jury deliberated in the jury room, the jury would be deadlocked and the twenty-two defendants would not be convicted.

"But if that happens, the district attorney can make us go through another trial, right?" said Washington.

"They won't do that in a misdemeanor case, right, Jourdane?" said Ladislao. "They don't want to spend that much money trying misdemeanors."

"What are misdemeanors?" Loo asked.

"Minor crimes," I responded. "You're charged with misdemeanors."

"So if one juror sticks with us, we win, right?" asked Ladislao.

"Normally, I'd agree with you, Lyle. But this isn't a normal case. This trial is very political. You should assume you'll be tried again if the jury is unable to reach a unanimous decision."

"How do they choose who is on the jury, Mr. Jourdane?" Loo asked.

"From the voter registration list and Department of Motor Vehicles records."

I told the students that we would receive a list of the potential jurors. The students could improve the chance of choosing a jury that would listen to their side by using the jury list, which is just names from the Registrar of Voters office. From that list they could find out where each potential juror lived, the juror's political party, and what petitions he or she had signed to put initiatives on the ballot. I told them it was all public information.

"Does that mean we can find out who on the jury list signed the anti-Vietnam intrusion measure?" asked Francisco.

"Yep. But so can the DA."

"And the nuclear power plant prohibition and the initiative to legalize marijuana?" laughed Spring Water.

"Uh huh."

"Pretty helpful information in choosing a jury in this kind of case," Loo grinned. "We can even drive by the potential jurors' houses and see what kinds of cars they own and if they have bumper stickers on them. We can talk to their neighbors and find out how the juror feels about minorities and the war."

"All that will help, but don't get too cocky," I cautioned. "You have a hard case to win."

"You might be right, Jourdane," said Ladislao, grinning at me, "but you're the one who's always saying we can win hard cases with lots of work and the belief we can do it."

The following Monday, friends and family of the defendants packed the courtroom. In the hallway outside the large wooden doors, television cameras rolled as the twenty-two youthful protesters entered Department One. Upon my advice, the students, like the young prosecutor, repeated into the microphones thrust inches from their lips, "no comment." Inside, reporters sat in readiness, pencils raised above notepads.

The bailiff ordered all to rise as the presiding judge entered the courtroom's rear door and took his seat on the bench four feet above everyone else in the room.

The county's chief prosecutor bolted to his feet. "Your Honor, in the interest of justice, the People request the Court dismiss the charges against these defendants."

That was it. It was all over.

Walking from the courtroom, Carol Loo wistfully told me she regretted missing the chance to take the witness stand and talk against the war and racial injustice.

"That's why the People dismissed the charges," I told her. "They didn't want you and your friends to talk on television about the war and Nixon invading Cambodia, violating international law and his duty to have Congress declare war, not to do so himself."

"I bet they didn't want us to talk about the police choosing to arrest minorities and not Whites, either," said Loo.

I reminded her that even though she missed the chance to exercise her right to free speech, she also missed an opportunity to spend the upcoming summer in jail.

Sixteen

IN THE SUMMER OF 1970, the Teamsters union was negotiating renewal of a contract for the truck drivers at most of the Salinas Valley ranches. During the truck driver negotiations, Teamster boss William Grami and Andrew Church, attorney for more than twenty-five growers in the Salinas Valley Growers Association, talked about the Teamsters becoming the exclusive bargaining agent for all field-workers the Salinas Valley growers used. A number of these growers had signed contracts with the United Farm Workers covering field-workers after César Chávez was victorious in the international grape boycott that ultimately forced Delano grape growers to negotiate with his union. The Teamsters represented truck drivers, not field-workers. The sole exception was at Bud Antle, where in 1961 the Teamsters signed a contract covering drivers and field-workers who were not hired to hoe or weed. As the California Supreme Court later noted, the 1961 Bud Antle and Teamster agreement might have been the result of company fears that Chávez was going to organize among Bud Antle workers.

Whatever the motivation behind the 1961 agreement between the Teamsters and Bud Antle, on July 23, 1970, the Salinas Valley growers ratified a new truck drivers' contract between the association members and the Teamsters. At that meeting, the association members decided to have a committee "feel out" the Teamsters on becoming the exclusive bargaining agent for all the association members' field-workers. The growers made no attempt to see how their workers felt about becoming members of the Teamsters. Apparently, to the growers this was not a relevant consideration. The next day, the Teamsters told the growers' committee they were receptive to the growers' offer that they represent the field-workers. The same day, the growers signed an agreement immediately recognizing the Teamsters as the bargaining representative for all field-workers. The Teamsters and the growers began bargaining, and within a few days entered a contract on behalf of all the field-workers. They agreed that for five years only the Teamsters could represent the workers and that all field-workers had to be Teamsters members to work for any of the twenty-five companies. Company foremen began signing workers up as Teamsters, telling them they would lose their jobs if they did not join. Most workers wanted to be represented by César Chávez and refused to join the Teamsters. On August 24, the UFW began a recognition strike against the companies. The companies stood by their contract with the Teamsters and sued the United Farm Workers to stop them from striking.

On September 21, Monterey County Superior Court Judge Gordon Campbell enjoined César Chávez and the United Farm Workers from striking. At Bud Antle's request, four days later the court added a prohibition on engaging in a secondary boycott. A secondary boycott occurs when, seeking to resolve nonviolently a volatile labor dispute, workers ask customers at a grocery store not to shop at the store because it sells a particular product the union is boycotting, such as grapes or lettuce. Judge Campbell ordered Chávez to notify all responsible persons that all boycott activities against Antle must cease. On November 9, the United Farm Workers appealed but the Monterey County judge ruled his order would remain in effect during the appeal unless the union posted a two-million-dollar bond, far more than the bond that rapists and robbers were required to file to be free pending trial. The workers continued to strike.

Shortly after I returned from lunch on December 4, a group of workers crowded into my tiny office.

"What's up?" I asked.

A Spanish voice replied. "As you know, last summer the growers entered into sweetheart contracts with the Teamsters Union."

"A sweetheart contract gives little or no benefit to the workers but says the union represents them and can force them to pay union dues, right?" I asked. I had no labor law experience.

"That's precisely what the Teamsters and the companies did."

"That gives the Teamsters Union a monopoly over food from the field to the market. Why would the growers do that?" I queried.

"To prevent us from having César Chávez and the United Farm Workers for our union," responded the group spokesman.

"I'd like to help you," I replied, "but since the lawyers I work for get money from the federal government, we can't represent the union."

"We are not here to ask you for help with our union, Señor Jourdane. You have shown us you are a friend of the farm worker. We saw you drive up to your office and we thought you'd like to know why all of us are over there," responded the spokesman, nodding toward several hundred farm workers massed outside the county jail visible from my office window. A year earlier, we had moved our office into an old house on Cayuga Street across the street from the courthouse.

The spokesman told me that César had come to Salinas to support the workers protesting the Teamsters' claim they represented the workers who were members of the United Farm Workers union and to protest the Teamster signing of a contract as the workers' union. When César went to the courthouse that morning, the police jailed the union leader until he complied with the order he was appealing. Like Mahatma Ghandi, César vowed to fast until he was released. Farm workers arrived from every part of California to hold a vigil.

While the workers and I spoke, Luis Jaramillo walked into my office. "You'll never believe it. Guess who Denny just got a call from?" Dennis Powell had become our directing attorney when he had transferred to Salinas a year earlier.

I shrugged my shoulders. "Richard Nixon?"

"Yeah, right. Teddy Kennedy." The Notre Dame law student told me that Bobby Kennedy's widow, Ethel, and Coretta King, Martin Luther King's widow, were coming to Salinas to visit César in jail. Kennedy wanted our office to do whatever it could to make sure Ethel's and Coretta's visit was safe.

"Good luck," I replied. "I don't think the people running this valley like the Kennedys or Coretta King much more than they like César Chávez."

That evening more than one thousand farm workers walked down dark Alisal Street from the United Farm Workers' office on Wood Street in east Salinas to the jail. When they reached the courthouse adjoining the building where César was a prisoner, they were jeered by scores of John Birch Society members and supporters wearing T-shirts embossed with the American flag. Jaramillo told me that what bothered him most was hearing shouts, "Communists, go back to Russia!" "Are we communists because we want to improve the life of farm workers?" Jaramillo asked. "I was born in Texas and am more American than those Birchers."

The next day, Mrs. Kennedy and Mrs. King flew into the tiny Salinas airport. Teamster goons, imported reportedly from Los Angeles, waited. Supporters of César Chávez, following his uncompromising belief in obtaining change through nonviolence, surrounded the two Eastern visitors and ignored the Teamster taunts and shoves. That afternoon, about thirty husky dock workers arrived to prevent the Teamsters from carrying out their threats on the nonviolent farm workers. The Teamsters stayed at the Travelers Inn on John Street. The dock workers stayed across the street. All night long downtown Salinas echoed with strong words of conflict. By morning all was quiet, as if the previous night's yelling had robbed the contestants of their voices. Farm workers continued to march through the valley, vowing to never join the Teamsters. César remained isolated in a tiny jail cell. Ethel Kennedy, Coretta King, the Los Angeles Teamster goons, and the dock workers went home.

César later said the visits from Ms. King and Ms. Kennedy "were great morale boosts for me, and I'm deeply thankful for them, but no matter how much support you have outside, a jail is still a jail."

Several weeks later, shortly before five p.m. and just two days before Christmas, the California Supreme Court issued a unanimous order that César Chávez be immediately freed from jail. Around 7:30, the union's chief organizer, Marshall Ganz, told the hundreds of farm workers gathered outside the jail that Monterey County Sheriff Jack Davenport had refused to release César until he had the order in his hand. Around 10:00, two union volunteers arrived in Salinas with the court order. When César walked from the jail in blue jail clothing, he heard the gathered farm workers singing the Mexican folksong "De Colores." Before attending mass, César told the farm workers, "It will soon be 2,000 years ago that the Prince of Peace was born and brought to the world the message that blessed are those who struggle for justice. It seems to me that those words say if you are fighting for justice, He'll be with you."

A year later, the California Supreme Court found unconstitutional the Monterey County court order that forced César Chávez to spend twenty days in jail just before Christmas in 1970.

Seventeen

EARLY ON THE MORNING after César was released from jail, Angie Valenzuela buzzed my office. "Mo, there's someone on the phone who wants to talk with you. He won't give his name."

I pushed the blinking button.

"Hi, Jourdane. This is Cohen. Can you meet with César?"

"Sure," I responded, excited to speak again with César's lawyer Jerry Cohen, who was developing a reputation as the best labor lawyer in the country, and with César Chávez, a man I had grown to revere.

"At noon, a Pontiac will park across the street from your office. Follow it when it pulls away from the curb. I'll explain when I see you."

I hung up imagining I was part of a James Bond thriller and about to meet Goldfinger. At 12:00, instead of going to the nearby La Revancha restaurant for my usual lunch, a burrito and a Coke, I drove out of the Rural Legal Assistance driveway. A dark Pontiac parked across the street pulled away from the curb. I followed. The Pontiac went down Market Street toward Castroville and after several turns headed back into Salinas. It followed the same anti-surveillance technique on Alisal Street and eventually pulled into a drive leading to several parking spaces behind a vacant storefront in a neglected Salinas neighborhood where many strawberry pickers and lettuce cutters lived. I watched the heavyset driver of the Pontiac walk to the rear door of the vacant building and knock. The door opened an inch, then several feet, allowing the Pontiac driver to squeeze through. I waited. Five minutes later, Jerry Cohen came out with a stocky companion he introduced as Marshall Ganz.

"Sorry to put you to all the hassle," said Cohen. "There've been threats on César's life, so we have to keep him hidden for now. We're returning to Delano in a few hours so he can spend Christmas with his family."

I entered the vacant building. It was a darkly shadowed room about the size of a handball court. Across the concrete floor, César Chávez lay in a hospital bed. Except for being slightly thinner, in the dim light he looked the same as when we had first met several years earlier in Delano. After offering his fast-weakened hand, César told me that he and Cohen had been talking about me.

"Have I done something wrong?" I asked defensively.

César smiled. "No. We want your help."

"I can't help the union, Mr. Chávez."

"But you can help union members," he responded. César told me that his members were afraid to go back to their jobs in the fields because of threatened Teamster violence.

"There's nothing I can do about that," I said, feeling helpless.

"But," said Cohen, "if an employee can avoid violence only by staying away from work, they are eligible for unemployment insurance. They don't have to make the impossible choice of starving their family or getting beat up."

"So what can I do?"

"Help them get unemployment insurance."

"Is the law on their side?" I asked, looking to Cohen for a response.

"Well," Cohen said hesitating, "César and I were talking about that. Didn't you win a case a few years ago in the federal court stopping the Employment Department from denying benefits to guys with long hair?"

"Yeah, employers claimed my clients made themselves unavailable for work by wearing their hair long, but that was different. I won because I was able to show my clients were expressing free speech through their long hair. One was a Native-American and the other a Vietnam Veteran Against the War."

"This will be easier. Just convince the judge not to make workers choose between being beaten and starving their children."

"If a client comes in, I'll do what I can."

"Will you do something else?" César asked.

I smiled. *The union always wants more*, I thought.

César told me that Jerry and his staff of Bill Carder, Chuck Farnsworth, and Frank Dennison were so busy fighting to stop the companies and Teamsters from destroying the union, they didn't have time to work on another serious problem.

"Didn't you tell me in Delano a few years ago that you wanted to do something about stoop labor?" César asked.

"Probably."

"Do you know that most farm workers you see stooped over in the field are thinning and weeding row crops?"

"Aren't row crops the ones that are planted in rows separated by foot-wide dirt canals to irrigate? Like lettuce and celery?"

"Yes. Do you know the workers are stooped over because the labor contractors and companies are forcing them to use the short hoe?"

I nodded.

Sipping his tea, César continued. "After you make sure striking workers who are afraid to return to their jobs are given their unemployment insurance benefits, will you get rid of the short hoe?" César asked bluntly.

"I wish I could."

"Why can't you?"

"A while back a client came in who wanted me to, but I had to refer him to a workers' compensation lawyer."

"Workers' compensation won't help farm workers with bad backs. Maybe you are too busy to handle this difficult case."

"I had to tell the man to see a private lawyer."

"Try to find the guy who wanted your help. I think you'll learn nothing has happened."

Walking to my car, I remembered the tired face of Sebastián Carmona. I had turned him away. There is a phrase in Spanish that can't really be translated into English, I thought, *me da vergüenza*. I guess the closest meaning in English is "I feel shame." I had many times before told myself that I would do anything to stop stoop labor and, when the chance walked through my door, I did nothing. With regret and embarassment, I had to admit to César Chávez, the founder of the first farm workers' union in history, that I had sent away a client who wanted help to stop the inhuman practice of forcing workers to do stoop labor. *Me da vergüenza.*

A few days after Christmas, Sebastián Carmona walked into the Soledad office. *"Señor Abogado,"* Carmona began shyly, apparently embarrassed to bother a lawyer again. He told me that he went to see the lawyer I had sent him to. He even took with him his boy who spoke English. The lawyer told him the courts would say that his kind of injury is not caused by his work. When the lawyer told him she could not help him, he thought there was no reason to bother me again. "I am glad you called my home," he said.

Eighteen

AFTER I PROMISED TO HELP CARMONA, Héctor asked if I realized how difficult it would be to get rid of the short-handled hoe. "Mo," he said, "agribusiness corporations have reasons for keeping the workers bent over with their faces in the dirt."

"Like?"

Héctor shook his head, apparently dismayed by my naiveté. "When a foreman forces the workers to bend over in order to keep control, what happens to his control if the workers stand up?"

I shrugged. Héctor shook his head.

"If you're denying your employees decent working conditions," he said, "decent pay, toilets in the field, medical care, vacations, pensions, and overtime pay when they work long hours, you'd better have something to keep the restless workers in line."

I stared at my friend.

"The Southern plantation owner used whips to control the black slaves," he said. "California corporations use short-handled hoes."

I spent the next two days researching in the Monterey County law library. After a weekend at the far more extensive Stanford law library, I decided I needed help. On Monday, I went to San Francisco to talk with Marty Glick.

"Have you found any law to help?" he asked.

"All I could come up with is a Department of Industrial Safety regulation that says, 'Hand tools shall be kept in good condition, and be safely stored. Unsafe hand tools shall not be used.'"

"That's not much law to get a court to change a hundred-year-old practice in California agriculture. You sure don't mess around choosing rickety windmills to fight, Jourdane."

I chuckled. "A hundred years isn't far off, Marty. At Stanford, I got tired of finding no law, so for something to do I looked at a treatise on agricultural history. Either Chinese or Japanese workers brought the short-handled hoe here in the nineteenth century. It seems that toward the end of the nineteenth century, the landowners in the Salinas Valley changed from growing wheat to growing row crops. I guess the price of wheat was too low because of the depression of the 1890s, but improvement in irrigation really favored growing row crops like lettuce and sugar beets. About the same time, lots of Chinese were available to do farm work because of completion of the railroads and the end of the Gold Rush. They became a cheap labor force and maybe they brought the short hoe."

"You said, maybe the Japanese brought it?"

"Some believe the short-handled hoe is a tool used in Japanese gardening, and that when the United States started importing Japanese workers around the turn of the century the Japanese brought the short-handled hoe to California. But they had a lot of freedom to choose what tool to use when farming and used both the long and short-handled hoe. After the Japanese workers started demanding better pay, the growers began using workers from Oklahoma and Mexico. By then the growers had learned that keeping control over the workforce was crucial for them to continue making huge profits. By making workers use the short hoe and stoop over all day, the growers kept control."

"You know the growers will say that workers do a better job with a short hoe than they could with a normal hoe," replied Glick.

"Probably, but I don't think there's that big of an advantage in using a short hoe. Even before the Civil War, the plantation owners in the South had the slaves use a normal hoe."

"The masters owned the slaves," said Glick. "If bending over all day disabled a slave, the cotton grower lost property."

"The corporations running the agribusiness industry still treat the workers like their property," I said.

"But now it's disposable property. When a worker becomes disabled, the corporation just hires a replacement from Mexico."

"Will you help me?" I asked.

"I've been wanting to get rid of the short-handled hoe since I came to Salinas. We can do it, Jourdane, but we need medical evidence showing use of the short hoe causes injury."

"Okay."

"And we need evidence showing that the incidence of back injuries is higher among farm workers than among other workers."

"It's gonna take years to gather the evidence you say we need," I moaned.

"If you want to change anything that's deeply rooted, Mo, you can't expect a quick fix."

Glick and I talked about combining a suit with an attack in the press and possibly getting the state assembly and senate to pass legislation, but even in this best-case scenario we would still face Governor Reagan's almost certain veto. Glick told me that whatever we decided to do, it would be hard, but we could win in the end because it was wrong to force workers to stoop over all day when it was not necessary to do the job. He added that in addition to evidence showing the short hoe caused workers to suffer pain and disability, we would also have to prove that use of the short hoe was not necessary to do the job.

Apparently thinking out loud, he said, "The key to this case might be in showing that the jobs workers are forced to do with the short hoe in Salinas are done in other places with a normal hoe." He suggested I continue to research the law and start amassing the evidence.

You always say we can do it, I thought. *Even with the right-wing courts and agencies, whether it's Judge Campbell or a Reagan-run state agency. You know that what is right will prevail if we prepare and are persistent.*

Driving home from San Francisco, my thoughts rambled.

When I had arrived in Hawaii twelve years earlier, a California surfer who was there to ride big waves, I thought reason and logic prevailed most of the time. Risks were worth taking. Some of my friends, mostly women, told me I took too many risks. Too often I paddled toward the darkening horizon, trying to crest mammoth swells before they broke. Too often, I didn't make it. Like the supreme court denying our prayer for a writ in the Ojeda case, Mother Nature on Oahu's north shore threw me and my board like an aphid on a twig into the cauldron of hundreds of tons of relentless white water. I always survived but was frequently reminded that there are forces a lot tougher than me. But since we were fighting to get rid of what was wrong, could we prevail?"

Around ten the next night, I walked out the front door of the Salinas Rural Legal Assistance office. Two guys were leaning against the driver's side of my VW bus.

"Pardon me," I said as I pulled out my keys.

"Hold yer horses, punk. We wanna talk to you."

Surprised, I looked up into the stony steel-gray eyes of a muscular man in his mid-twenties. "What?" I asked in a bewildered tone.

"I said we want to talk to you," repeated one of the skinheads, rubbing his knuckles.

"What'a ya want?" I managed to ask firmly, as if unaffected by the churning fear swelling inside me.

"Don't fuck with us," growled the butch-cut blond.

"What?" I responded.

"You don't know shit about farming. You're a lawyer. Don't try to tell us how to grow the crops. Stick to your books. We'll handle the fields."

"What're you talking about?"

"Don't fuck with us, dude," said the shorter man, pushing my shoulder, knocking me against the side of the bus. "You heard my buddy. You do and you're dead."

Abruptly, the two walked to a pickup and pulled away.

Like a teen who does the opposite of what his mother says, the bullies' effort to abort my desire to ban the short-handled hoe had the opposite effect.

The *cortito* forced workers unnecessarily to spend hours stooped in the field to thin and weed crops. It became the symbol of growers' dominance over farm workers, like the whip in the South before the Civil War. (Valley of the World Agriculture Exhibition, courtesy of National Steinbeck Center Archives, Sam Vestel)

Farm workers stoop with the *cortito* in a Salinas Valley, sugar beet field. (Valley of the World Agriculture Exhibition, courtesy of National Steinbeck Center Archives, Sam Vestel)

United Farm Workers' members across the Salinas and Pajaro Valleys
when the growers entered into sweetheart contracts with the Teamsters.
(Valley of the World Agriculture Exhibition, courtesy of National
Steinbeck Center Archives, Sam Vestel)

In the model of Chávez's nonviolence, United Farm Workers from the
edge of a field near Watsonville, CA, peacefully urge replacement to
join the strikers. (Valley of the World Agriculture Exhibition, courtesy
of National Steinbeck Center Archives, Sam Vestel)

Farm workers in scorching San Joaquin Valley field. (Courtesy of former CRLA attorney W.B. Daniels, 1970)

After a day stooped in the fields, bracero workers await dinner outside the dining room of the Gondo Watsonville Labor Camp. (Valley of the World Agriculture Exhibition, courtesy of National Steinbeck Center Archives, Sam Vestel)

Despite their difficult life, the smiles on the faces of San Joaquin Valley farm workers' children and their proud father reveal an inner strength rarely seen on city streets. (Courtesy of former CRLA attorney W.B. Daniels, 1967)

Dolores Huerta on a picket line in the San Joaquin Valley in 1967. She and César Chávez founded the National Farm Workers Association in 1962 that eventually became the United Farm Workers union, AFL-CIO. (Courtesy of George Ballis/Take Stock, 1976)

César Chávez discussing farm workers' problems in the Salinas Valley with CRLA community workers Héctor De la Rosa and Enrique Cantú Flores. (Courtesy of former CRLA attorney W.B. Daniels, 1970)

When the Gonzalez School Board fired teacher Paula Álvarez because she encouraged students from farm work-er families to attend college, Ralph Abascal and CRLA filed suit in the federal court. (Courtesy of former CRLA attorney W.B. Daniels, 1970)

Maurice Jourdane seeks to resolve amicably a dispute between United Farm Workers and a market in Hollister during the grape boycott. (Courtesy of Kathleen Jourdane, 1969)

Farm workers mass outside the Monterey County Courthouse in Salinas awaiting the release of César Chávez who was incarcerated for leading a nonviolent boycott of lettuce after the growers signed sweetheart contacts with the Teamsters against the workers' desire to continue membership in César's union. (Valley of the World Agriculture Exhibition, courtesy of National Steinbeck Center Archives, Sam Vestel)

In the mid-1960s, attorney John Cohen left the MacFarland CRLA office to become the lawyer for César Chávez and the United Farm Workers. Here, Cohen is explaining to a group of Delano workers their right to picket on a public road. (Courtesy of former CRLA attorney W.B. Daniels, 1967)

With his bushy hair and optimistic spirit, Mo Jourdane begins working as a law student in Delano in 1967. (Courtesy of Mo Jourdane, passport photo, 1972)

Marty Glick stopped growers from using guest workers to take jobs from United States residents, and the State of California from labeling farm workers' children mentally retarded because they scored low on English-administered IQ tests. His efforts at CRLA also helped to stop growers from forcing workers to stoop in the field with the short-handled hoe. (Courtesy of former CRLA attorney W.B. Daniels, 1968)

CALIFORNIAN

WEATHER
SALINAS VALLEY
Variable clouds through
tomorrow with variable winds.
Rainfall yesterday .00. Season total
11.99.
High yesterday 54. This morn-
ing's low 42.
(Complete Forecast on Page 11.)

RNIA, MONDAY AFTERNOON, APRIL 7, 1975

Three Sections • 15 Cents

Its ft'

says 747 onto
ng rain.
ho forbade the
ng too close to
hom were in-
t, because Mrs.
ider cancer
weakens her
n. However, she
t.
n were kept
e they were
pneumonia, in-
tion. Dr. Alex
peared to be
on't expect any

eration Babylift
Doctors, nurses
ared to tend the
lift nursery and
San Francisco
ens across the
pt the children.
ers who made it
were all spoken

C141 Starlifters
ay, carrying 132
Page 12

iell age iigon

— Communist
torage area less
n the center of
the first major
since the start of

had shifted the
fensive around
Mekong Delta,
said the North
Cong carried out
n six previ-
ty reported at

Farmworker crouches over now illegal hoe in field off Blanco Road.

In April 1975, after the Supreme Court found substantial medical evidence that the short-handled hoe caused farm workers permanent back injury, the California Industrial Safety Board held hearings around the state. The Salinas *Californian* followed efforts to ban the *cortito*. (Courtesy of the Salinas *Californian*, 1975)

During the early seventies, in retaliation to CRLA diligently protecting the rights of farm workers, Governor Ronald Reagan sought to close the federal legal services program. After hearings before Supreme Court justices from across the country, Reagan's charges of wrongdoing by the lawyers were found groundless. (Courtesy of the Salinas *Californian*)

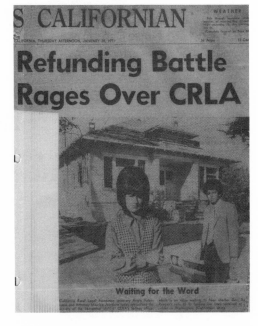

S CALIFORNIAN

CALIFORNIA, THURSDAY AFTERNOON, JANUARY 28, 1971

Refunding Battle Rages Over CRLA

Waiting for the Word

California Supreme Court rules short-handled hoe causes irreparable back injury. —News Item.

Because the short-handled hoe causes permanent disability, slaves were not forced to use hoes as short as those forced on Hispanic farm workers in California. (Courtesy of Tribune Media Services, Paul Conrad, published in *LA Times*, 1975)

Nineteen

SEVERAL WEEKS LATER I was in the Imperial Valley. While there, Derek Weston, the CRLA attorney, told me he knew a doctor who saw patients at a farm workers' clinic in Brawley, an overwhelmingly Mexican-populated community twenty miles north of the Mexican border. With its one-room courthouse and one block of small stores, Brawley was about as large as any town in the Imperial Valley. The adobe buildings on Main Street, with its covered sidewalk, reminded me of Oaxaca. The doctor's office, a small converted home, sat a block off Main on one of the city's several residential avenues. After a short wait in the tiny reception room packed with coughing *campesinas* and tightly held runny-nosed toddlers, I felt guilty when the young receptionist told me the doctor could talk with me.

I walked into physician David Flanagan's office and apologized for bothering him when so many sick patients needed him. He chuckled at my offer to return when he wasn't so busy, reminding me there weren't many doctors caring for farm-worker patients in Brawley. The young general practitioner sat patiently while I rapidly explained our attempt to ban the short-handled hoe.

He stopped me. "Mr. Jourdane. I've been here for over two years. Every day, I see farm workers in the fields. I'm glad someone else finally noticed they're stooped over. Millions of people drive past stooped farm workers, and no one seems to care what bending over all day does to a person's back."

"Can you explain in lay terms what it does?" I opened an 8½ by 13 inch yellow legal pad and scribbled rapidly, trying not to miss anything Dr. Flanagan said.

"It's not that hard to explain. Our spine is a stack of bones called vertebrae. They're piled on top of one another. Between the vertebrae are soft discs, like Jell-O sealed in a plastic bag. I don't care who you are or what you do, when you bend over all day, the discs in your spine degenerate. In time a disc herniates or explodes."

"Does that happen to all of us when we bend over?"

"It can. Your discs don't care if you're an African-American janitor scrubbing floors or a Mexican-American farm worker weeding lettuce. Over our lifetime, our spine's discs degenerate. But you and I don't spend all day bending over."

"Like farm workers."

Doctor Flanagan smiled. "Even though a farm worker might have an attractive thirty-year-old face, the same worker forced to do stoop labor has the spine of a seventy-year-old. By the time too many farm workers are forty, they're disabled and unable to work."

Crossing the Pajaro Valley between my home in Aptos and my office in Salinas, I drove through lettuce fields. Every morning my stomach tightened and my pulse raced when I passed crews of small bodies bent over with their heads to the ground, arms rhythmically raising and lowering a short-handled hoe. Every morning I felt the bitterness of the workers' suffering, knowing when they walked from the field that evening they would have one less day before being crippled by a herniated spinal disc. More than once, approaching Salinas Avenue after reaching the hill from the straight rows of lettuce in the valley, my eyes moistened with sadness. I vowed over and over, "With your help, God, we can do it. With your help and our persistence, we can stop that torture in our fields. I place my trust in you, God."

In the winter, it seems like it rains most of the time in Salinas. One evening, on the local news I heard the president of Pik n' Pak, the corporation that took over Salinas Strawberries, tell the reporter that he regretted that all the fine Mexican families had to move from the company's housing, but he was sure they could return to their homes in Mexico until next season. Closing the housing was purely a business decision.

"I can't believe it," I mumbled to Kathy in our warm home. "The company is throwing over a hundred children into the muddy street."

The next morning seven drenched farm workers sloshed into our office. "*Abogado*, we have to talk with you," announced one in a clear Spanish voice.

I walked with the workers to find Denny Powell, who was now director of the office. After Denny arranged chairs for the anxious farm workers, Sixto Torres, the spokesman, told us the company had evicted everybody, more than sixty families.

"Did they tell you why?" I asked.

"They're closing the housing. Since the season is over, they no longer need us. They do not care that our children must leave their schools and will be without a home."

"What are you going to do?" Denny asked.

"We've already done it. We're living in the street outside the camp. We see our homes empty and locked just a few feet from where we sleep in the rain. We have nowhere to go."

Denny and I rode with Sixto to talk with the families living on the mud shoulder of Natividad Road. By 9 A.M., we waited on hard chairs in the reception area outside the office of the company president. Around 9:30, he wandered in, glanced at us, and entered his private office. He closed his office door firmly. At 10:00, the receptionist said the president would see us.

"What can I do for you, Mr. Powell?" asked the gray-haired chief executive officer, staring harshly through his horn-rimmed bifocals.

"We're here on behalf of the families in the street." Carefully choosing his words, Denny tried to encourage the company executive to feel the anguish caused by closing the camp with no notice.

The company chief executive was firm. "The decision to close the housing is final. Destruction crews are on their way to tear the shacks down."

Denny and I went outside and reported the company's position to the families. Over and over I heard, "We have nowhere to go."

I spent the morning calling the City of Salinas and Monterey County, trying to get portable toilets installed on the road where the workers were living. The government bureaucrats all refused my request, one admitting they did not want to get involved in a union fight. Finally, I called the director of Rural Legal Assistance, Cruz Reynoso.

"Get toilets installed," ordered Reynoso. "We'll get the money to pay for them somewhere. Let me worry about that. Spend your time finding the people housing. We can't let them live in the street."

The following evening, Denny Powell and I appeared at a city council meeting. In a room overflowing with farm worker families, on behalf of those families Powell explained the problem to the five elected officials. He reminded the city council that there were about seven open parks in the town. He asked the council to allow the families to stay in one of the parks for a very short period until they found other housing.

The council recessed to talk behind closed doors. It returned shortly. "Mr. Powell, we have considered your request. We recognize your problem. I recommend you advise your clients to return to their homes in Mexico. They will be welcome to return next summer for the season. Our parks are for our children's recreation. We don't need a bunch of . . . of homeless migrants filling them with their litter. Your request is denied."

The all-white male council members abruptly stood up and scurried through the rear exit. I was not surprised. I walked out angry and frustrated behind the sad farm worker families.

When Toribio Ortega, the community worker who had replaced Manuel Olivas, translated for the Spanish-speaking families what the city council had decided, I heard a mother weep, "Our children are citizens of this country. They have lived here their whole lives."

I heard a father curse, "We no longer have a house in Mexico. Doesn't the *pinchi* city council know we live in America? Will the *güeros* never let us stop stooping and stand tall?"

The next morning I arrived at the office to find a message for the first attorney to arrive: call the county sheriff. Being the first in the office that morning, I answered the sheriff's call immediately.

"Good morning," responded the deep voice. "After I heard Mr. Powell at the city council meeting last night, I talked with several of the council members. I think you'll like the good news I have for you."

My hopes skyrocketed. Holding the phone to my ear, I felt like a sixteen-year-old in Mazatlán dropping into a wave on my thirty-pound, nine-foot board. The swell rose far over my head, a glassy green wall lay ahead.

In fact, the sheriff's news was good. Hanging up, I quickly walked out of the office to my VW bus. When I arrived at the camp on the side of the muddy road, a middle-aged woman with her small grandchildren surrounded my Volkswagen. "*Señor abogado*," she said urgently, "some growers' kids hit Sixto's wife with a truck last night. Sixto wants to see you."

I found Sixto Torres huddled with several *compadres* behind a pickup truck. A glimpse at Sixto's face and I knew the brawny six-foot-three-inch frame held back a ready-to-burst reservoir of anger. Walking from the gathering crowd, the homeless farm worker slowly explained in his perfect Spanish, "Early this morning, while my wife walked on the side of the road, a pickup came barreling down the street. It hit her after it swerved over the line along the edge of the road. It did not even stop. Mendoza's kids recognized the driver."

"Who was it?" I asked, jotting down Sixto's words on a legal pad.

"A white guy they know from work."

"Did you call the police?" I asked Sixto.

"Sure. They came and took a report, but they will do nothing."

"Is your wife okay?" I asked.

"She's at the hospital. The truck was going very fast."

"What I'm here to ask you is not important now," I muttered, "but I guess I have to tell you what the city council decided."

"I already know, *abogado*. Do you forget I was there last night?"

"No," I stuttered. "I, I mean yes, I remember. I know you were there, but there is more." Speaking very slowly and carefully, hoping the families would understand my Spanish, I translated the sheriff's offer. "The council has reconsidered your request. You may stay temporarily, and the council members asked the sheriff to stress the word temporarily, at the sewage disposal site south of town."

When I gave the workers the sheriff's message, Sixto chuckled bitterly. "Let me meet with the other families. I will call you, *abogado*." An hour later, I was back in my cozy office. Sixto Torres was on the line calling from a pay phone a half mile from the Salinas Strawberry housing. "We have a response to the sheriff's offer," he said. "Do you have a pencil?"

"Uh huh," I responded, searching for a pen through the files strewn across my desk.

"Tell them we have considered their offer. We say, write this part down, 'No, thank you. For years you treat us like walking manure while we work in your fields growing food to feed your families. We can do nothing about how badly you treat us. But we will never allow our children to sleep in your shit.'"

During the eight years that followed, Sixto Torres would not give up. Christmas came and thirty-two families remained in the street. The others either found somewhere to stay locally or returned to Mexico. Finally, through Sixto's persistent calls to the county housing authority, it reopened an old labor camp on Old Stage Road northeast of Salinas that had housed Japanese workers around the turn of the century when *braceros* were used to replace local workers. It had been vacant since the Bracero Program had ended.

Not long after the homeless farm workers moved in, suddenly, for $22,000, the housing authority sold the camp out from under them. On behalf of the thirty-two families, Sixto began negotiating to buy the camp from the new buyer, Leo Briggs. Near the end of 1972, Briggs sold the displaced workers the camp for $110,000. By 1979, through the workers' own labor; the counseling of Dave Kirkpatrick, a Harvard law school graduate who had joined our Salinas office as head of CRLA's housing task force; and Ed Moncrief, who was with the Central Coast Counties Corporation, the former Pic n Pac workers had rebuilt the decrepit labor camp into family homes.[1]

---

[1]This monumental achievement was additionally facilitated by financial assistance from the Catholic Campaign and the Farmers Home Administration.

Twenty

WITHIN A COUPLE MONTHS after I began working in Salinas, my weekly trip thirty miles south to Soledad had become a daily task. Each evening, farm workers walked through the door with legal problems. Around 1970, Héctor convinced our bosses in San Francisco to spend $90 a month of the limited federal money California Rural Legal Assistance received on rent for a small corner office on Oak Street. After the last client departed one evening, sitting in our barren two-room office, Héctor and I found a minute to talk about the investigation he had been conducting for the short-handled hoe case.

"Almost every farm worker in the Salinas Valley over fifty has a permanently disabling back injury," he said. "Three out of four over forty are permanently disabled."

"Both men and women?"

"Both men and women."

"What do the companies say about that?"

"That the back injuries are due to the farm workers' hard life generally," responded Héctor, "not just the short-handled hoe."

"Maybe," I pondered. "We need to find out about the incidence of disabling back injuries among farm workers in areas where they don't use the short hoe."

"My dad says they didn't use it in Michigan when he was a *bracero* there," said Héctor. "And they didn't use it in Texas, New Mexico, or Arizona. I didn't see a short-handled hoe until I got to Salinas."

"Héctor, why don't you check with the other CRLA offices. See if they have a high incidence of back injuries in their areas. I'll find out where the short hoe is used and where it isn't."

A week later, I was in the Salinas office when Héctor phoned. He had called all the offices from Marysville and Santa Rosa in the north to the Imperial Valley in the south. Back injuries were a problem among farm workers in areas where they grow row crops like lettuce, celery, and sugar beets, but not in areas where farm workers work around trees like citrus, peach, or walnut.

"Because farm workers don't use the *cortito* around trees," I said.

"You're learning, Mo," Hector replied.

Following Marty Glick's earlier suggestion, I continued to research the law. When I was still unable to find anything helpful besides the regulation that prohibited unsafe hand tools, I pursued Glick's other suggestion that it would not be enough to show use of the short hoe caused back injury. Surely, we could not convince a court that the regulation made the use of a knife illegal, because bending over to use the knife to cut lettuce was the only way to cut the lettuce. If we wanted to ban the short-handled hoe, we had to show that there was a safe alternative method to thin and weed crops. I recalled Héctor and the evicted Pic n' Pac workers saying they had used the long hoe to thin and weed before coming to California. I went to talk with Sixto Torres. Meanwhile, Glick talked with Los Angeles attorney Mickey Kantor, who was connected with progressive legal networks across the country, about getting contacts in the South. Soon, Marty handed me a list of the directors of legal service projects throughout the United States.

In August, 1971, I wrote to every legal service program in the United States, from Maine to Hawaii, from Washington to Florida. I told them that California Rural Legal Assistance was concerned with the use of the short-handled hoe to thin and weed crops in parts of California and it would be helpful to know whether this work was done elsewhere with the long-handled hoe. I asked them to complete a sheet I attached and return it to me. On the sheet, I asked: the geographical area covered by their office, what crops were harvested in their area, whether some clients engaged in farm work, whether they used a hoe, whether it had a long handle (approximately five feet) or a short handle (approximately fifteen inches), and, if both long- and short-handled hoes were being used, which crops were done with the long hoe and which with the short hoe?

I received sixty-two responses. Outside of California all thinning and weeding was done with the long-handled hoe.

Talking one afternoon with Susan Alva, CRLA's community worker in our Ceres office near Modesto, I learned that the long-handled hoe was used in the San Joaquin Valley to thin and weed crops. Susan was an immigrant to the San Joaquin Valley, having grown up in Hollywood with her Dominican family. Just out of high school, she left Los Angeles and attended Stanislaus State College with many children of farm workers who were the new generation of Latinos in California. She began working with California Rural Legal Assistance attorneys Gene Livingston, Jim Mattisich, and Manny Medeiros. Later, she went on to work as an organizer for the United Farm Workers in the Imperial Valley. Eventually, Susan became an attorney and is today a strong advocate for immigrants in Los Angeles. As a young community worker, Susan went to the fields around Modesto and photographed farm workers using the long-handled hoe to weed sugar beets. Evidence.

Like all CRLA attorneys, I was seeing around twenty new clients a week. Each case took time, so my availability to work on the short-handled hoe case was limited. To each client, their case was the most important one in the world. I spent many Saturdays and many late nights at the office trying to make time to work on the short-handled hoe case. Before the year ended, I went to San Francisco to talk with Glick about the information he, Héctor, and I had accumulated.

"Think it's enough to file a petition?" I asked.

After looking at the notes I had taken from my interviews with three doctors and scribbled statistics based upon what Héctor and I had learned, Glick told me we needed to talk with more doctors to make sure the short-handled hoe caused the injury Flanagan said it caused. We also needed a formal survey comparing the incidence of permanently disabling back injuries among farm workers who used the short hoe compared with those who did not.

"I can talk to more farm workers and doctors," I said, "but our clients don't have the money to pay for a formal survey."

"We need something in black and white showing that workers who use the short hoe suffer permanently disabling back injuries far more frequently than those who don't," said Glick.

"I can't believe with all the time we've spent on this case we'll have to give up because we can't afford crucial evidence," I moaned.

"Welcome to the world of lawyers, Jourdane. Far too many cases are lost because a party doesn't have the money to pay lawyers, much less for evidence needed to prove the case. Stay positive. We'll get a formal survey somewhere."

I walked in shock through the light San Francisco rain to my car. Weaving through the freeway traffic on the way home, the burden of how to get money to pay for the needed survey pressed hard on my mind. I thought about César Chávez. "*Sí se puede,*" he would say, "You can do it." Knowing Chávez had been forced to work with the short hoe as a young man, I stopped in San Jose to see the physician treating his low-back injury. I wasn't surprised when the San Jose doctor told me stoop labor had destroyed César's back.

Twenty-one

FOR WEEKS AFTER GLICK recommended I obtain a formal survey showing farm workers who used the short-handled hoe had a higher incidence of back disability than those who did not, I scoured the state's records on disabilities and tried to raise money to pay for the study. Finally, one Friday evening I stopped by the Mission Street pool hall in Santa Cruz where Ladislao Piñeda worked evenings.

"Lyle," I asked while he sat behind the counter holding a paperback, "know anyone who will do a study on farm workers for me for free?"

"Maybe. Tell me what you want and when you want it, and I'll find someone at the university. One of my professors, Ralph Guzmán, really wants to help you get rid of the *cortito*. Let me talk to him. Plus, students at UCSC owe you a lot for keeping them out of jail a couple of years ago."

With the help of Dr. Guzmán, a month later the University of California students handed me a formal survey showing that the incidence of permanently disabling back injuries among farm workers in an area where they used the short hoe was 15.6 percent. It was only 3.7 percent, by comparison, where farm workers did not use the short-handled hoe.

Meanwhile, we had gotten declarations or sworn statements from a sample of farm workers who used the short-handled hoe and from six physicians describing the effect of the short hoe on farm workers' backs.

When Héctor asked if I was finally ready to file the suit to ban the short-handled hoe, I replied, "Yep, but I don't know who to sue. If I sue Carmona's employer, I stop it only at one ranch, even if I win. I could spend the rest of my life suing growers one by one to stop them from making their workers do unnecessary stoop labor."

The next day I called Glick. "The Industrial Safety Board has the statutory duty to enforce the law we're relying on," he reminded me. "We'll file our petition with them. If we convince them the growers are breaking the law by making workers use the short hoe, they can stop its use and we win."

"And if they don't?" I asked.

Twenty-two

WITH DECLARATIONS SIGNED and sworn to by farm workers who were disabled after using the short hoe and doctors who treated them, letters from legal service programs nationwide showing the long-handled hoe was used safely throughout the United States to do the exact same work farm workers were forced to use the short-handled hoe to do in California, and the University of California survey, Glick and I were ready to file the petition. The morning I left home in Aptos for Glick's San Francisco office, Kathy kissed me good-bye and said, "I love Marty's idea about filing a petition with the Industrial Safety Board, but I doubt that the Reagan-appointed board is even going to listen to your case. It's too political. You guys are asking conservatives for too big a change in the status quo. It's like Abe Lincoln asking Jefferson Davis to free the slaves."

While Kathy questioned our chances, Glick, now CRLA's new director, and I decided we should try to resolve the dispute through a petition to the Industrial Safety Board. If they denied our petition, we could seek review in the courts that still had many of the humane justices appointed by former Governor Pat Brown.

On September 20, 1972, Glick and I began stacking the petitions and voluminous attachments for our trek several blocks away to the San Francisco office of the Industrial Safety Board. With the petition, we filed the declaration of José Romero swearing he had worked with the short-handled hoe for ten years. José felt that stoop labor caused by the short hoe was the most difficult and lowest paying job in the state. He told the Board, "We farm workers who make our living out working in the fields find ourselves having to return to work every day with backs, necks, and legs that still hurt from working the day before.

I do not wish to work with the short handle. It is not a human type of job. No one should be expected to work bent down for that length of time. Short-handled hoe work is too hard to do. The short-handled hoe ruins the farm worker's back before he is fifty; he is so disabled he must go on welfare."

Eligio de Haro, also a farm worker, was forty-one years old when he told the Board, "I first worked with the *cortito* in 1965 in Calexico, California. I had worked in New Mexico with a long handle, thinning and weeding cotton. I could easily work for ten hours a day with a long handle. When I worked with the *cortito* I find it hard to work eight hours. I come home with so much pain sometimes rubbing and hot patches don't help."

Jesús Serrano had been a farm worker his entire life. In the winter of 1968–1969 he became disabled. He could no longer bend over. He told the Board, "During my working years my friends used to make fun of me because of the way I walked, bent forward like a gorilla, which is caused by working with a *cortito*."

Sebastián Carmona told the Board, "As the years went by I began to realize that I wasn't walking as erect as before. I definitely feel that using the short-handled hoe was responsible for weakening me to the point that I can no longer sit or stand straight as I once did. I am forty-six years old."

Isabel Cardena told the Board she was unable to endure the pain caused by the short hoe. She said, "When there is no other work available but the *cortito*, my oldest son is the only one that can work and provide for us. It is also hard for him; he is only sixteen, but he has no choice."

Juan López told the Board he was disabled. He could no longer bend over. He and his family were compelled to migrate "to Idaho and Washington every year during the short-handled hoe season, because there they use long-handled hoes."

With the petition we also filed affidavits or declarations from five physicians. Doctor Flanagan told the Board that prolonged use of the short-handled hoe caused pain and permanent back injuries. Doctor Mizrahi of the San Joaquin Valley told the Board he was familiar with the short-handled hoe: the posture required to use the tool resulted in tissue injury and severe back pain. He said that "a frequent long range result [was] degeneration of the intervertebral discs and supporting ligaments of the spine, resulting in pain, lack of ability to move freely," and in many cases complete disability. Doctors F. R. Williams of Mountain View; David Brooks, who specialized in treating farm workers; C. Arthur Spalding, an orthopedic surgeon from Monterey; and Dr. Jerry Lackner, who treated farm workers in Delano (and was later appointed by Governor Jerry Brown as director of the California Department of Health), agreed with Mizrahi and Flanagan: As Lackner saw it, requiring workers to spend the day stooped over with a short-handled hoe caused degeneration of the spine's discs and supporting ligaments and, in many cases, permanent disability.

Several months after we filed the petition, a secretary for the Industrial Safety Board called. When Angie buzzed my office and told me who was on the line, I felt as powerless as a husband watching his wife suffer through the last days of metastasis of breast cancer. Everyone had convinced me the Reagan-selected Safety Industrial Board, which had done nothing to encourage industrial safety, would dismiss the petition outright. I shakily picked up the receiver, prepared for the rejection of the farm workers' petition.

Twenty-three

"WE HAVE SCHEDULED A HEARING in San Francisco for March 6 on your petition," the Industrial Safety Board employee told me in a soft voice. "At the hearing, we expect to hear from witnesses on both sides of the issue you raise. You will receive notice of the hearing in the mail."

I immediately called Glick. The more experienced lawyer listened. I rambled.

"I'll tell you, Mo," Glick said after I calmed down, "I expected the Industrial Safety Board to dismiss the petition without taking testimony."

"Now we'll have a trial and the agribusiness industry has millions of dollars to spend on lawyers to grind us into the ground."

"But we'll beat 'em in the end," Glick responded. "We have hope. Unlike growers who look at change as threatening, we know we can change things for the better. And our clients learned long ago to patiently endure and persist. If we lose before the Board, we'll go to court. If we lose there, we'll go to another court. We have persistence, Jourdane. Someday, the workers will win this one. It may not happen now. Maybe not next year. But someday the workers in the Salinas Valley will no longer have to bend over all day to do a job they can do standing erect."

For the next two months, I traveled throughout the state talking with farm workers who wanted to tell of their experience working with the short hoe. On March 6, 1973, the Board held its first hearing in San Francisco. Doctor David Flanagan testified:

After completing medical school at Georgetown University in Washington, D.C., I spent four years specializing in surgery, the last two years of which were spent exclusively in orthopedic surgery at the Cornell University Medical Center in New York City, at the hospital for special surgery. After leaving New York, I helped to organize and operate a clinic for migrant and seasonal farm workers in the Imperial Valley of California, and it is there that I spent more than two years dealing with the problems of the farm workers. From the outset I began to see what I considered an inordinately high percentage of low back conditions.

Dr. David Flanagan told the Board that it became apparent to him the type of manual labor performed by farm workers was responsible for the development of many symptoms in and about the spine. There was almost invariably a prior history of regular use of the short-handled hoe. Flanagan became convinced that use of the short-handled hoe was an unnecessary contributing factor to the premature degeneration of the structures of the low back regions and if the short-handled hoe could be modified in some way or eliminated from use,

this would contribute considerably to the overall better prognosis of those who already had sustained or who could be expected to sustain injuries or develop symptoms in the low back region. My contention is that if the farm worker is able to stand erect using a tool which does not require the hyper-flexion of the spine, that much of the pathology which I see at the clinic could be eliminated or delayed by changing the stresses which when applied to this region of the spine create a progressive degeneration or wearing out of the structure of the low back.

After Flanagan described the anatomical structure of the spine at some length and exhibited a model and some X-rays, he attested to the following:

This is a progressive process, a gradual wearing out that everybody goes through. There are no shortcuts. The body just gradually wears out and these structures do not regenerate. It's just part of getting old. Most of us avoid problems in this area. This, however, is not the case for farm workers, especially those using the short hoe. They are subject to unusual stresses and strains with an increasing degeneration or wearing out of these structures. With repeated injury and insult to these structures, the wearing process accelerates and there is no regeneration . . . and therefore there is no medical cure, merely a patching up or slowing down of an ongoing process of degeneration. The ligaments become ragged, irregular, and denuded of their smooth articulating surfaces. The discs become more brittle, with cracks and hardening or seepage of the liquid centers, which then bulge and apply pressure on the nearby nerves to the lower extremities. The bones fracture in some cases and the fractures do not heal. The results of the degeneration of these structures are seen as distinct clinical entities and are most often not the result of a single severe injury but rather are the result of repeated continuous small injuries to the structures which allows for the development of clinical pathology over a varying period of time. I cannot emphasize enough the importance of the concept that these conditions develop as a result of repeated small injuries over a period of years and usually are not the result of a single severe on-the-job accident. One does not develop arthritis or a "slipped disc," to use the common term, or develop spondylolisthesis as a result of the particular injury which is often associated with acute onset of symptoms in the performance of a certain job. The particular injury is more the case of the straw that broke the camel's back, rather than the sole responsible cause for the symptoms.

I hope I can explain to you the role that the use of the short hoe has in the development of these clinical conditions, which are commonly seen in the farm worker. I feel that the role is primarily one of position, specifically a malpositioning of the body, which through stressing the low back structures allows for continued and repeated insults and injuries which we know are necessary and responsible for the development of clinical symptoms. I think we all realize what a great amount of effort and money has gone into the education of the manual laboring force in the proper positioning of the body when doing heavy labor, particularly concerning proper lifting techniques. This campaign of safety with regard to lifting is directed primarily at the protection of the low back structure and has been very successful in decreasing the number of work injuries to the back. As you know, the basis of this campaign is the maintenance of the back in an erect position with optimal alignment of the spine while using the power of the lower extremities to do the lifting. It is obvious that the correct positioning of the spine is important in order to avoid injury and it is the malpositioning of the spine that is necessary in order to use the short hoe.

One might be tempted to say that the spine may not be in an optimal position when using the short hoe, but there is no weight involved in the work being done, but this is simply not the case. For an average 170-pound male in this position, the muscles are actually lifting more than 90 pounds every second. If you multiply that times the number of seconds in that position for an eight- or ten-hour day, it represents thousands of pounds daily and it is easy to see that this significant amount of weight is being applied to the spine at the very point where most degeneration occurs and most symptoms develop. The pelvis, including the sacrum, which is the joint at which the spine attaches to the weight-bearing structures of the lower extremities, is fixed like a fulcrum point while forces and motion occur at the adjacent non-fixed point at the lowest part of the spine, specifically the lower lumbar area. And these shearing forces are applied to this portion of the spine while it is almost 90 degrees away from its normal weight-bearing position. Besides this shearing force, we should not forget the hundreds of pounds of compressing forces applied horizontally to the vertebrae and the discs just to maintain the body in this unusual position. It is no accident, therefore, that symptoms and clinical conditions develop at the juncture of the lumbar spine and the sacrum and this is indeed statistically where most disease develops, for example, 90 percent of the disc disease develops at the L-5 S-1 level and this is also true of the development of spondylolisthesis and is generally true of degenerative osteoarthritis as well.

There is no doubt in my mind that the short hoe plays a very important and significant role in the development of pathology of the low back region and should be considered a [major] health hazard . . . to the portion of the population which is required to use this tool.

Board member Albert Turner asked Dr. Flanagan, ". . . [L]et's assume that a man forty-five years old has spent ten years working in fields with a short hoe. Would you dare to guess how much more likely he would be to have back problems than a guy that wasn't, that didn't use the short hoe?"

Dr. Flanagan responded, "I think it would exceed one hundred percent. Anybody that's been using the short hoe extensively in the field over a ten-year period has got back trouble."

The Board having heard uncontroverted evidence that use of the short-handled hoe caused farm workers to suffer pain and resulted in permanent disability, and nothing to the contrary, I naively assumed it had to find the short hoe an unsafe hand tool. But when the San Francisco hearing ended, the Board told Glick and me that we were raising an interesting issue and it needed to hear additional evidence.

"What did you expect?" Glick asked when we talked after the hearing. "How many times do you need to hear that the Industrial Safety Board is appointed by Governor Reagan. They aren't going to ban the short-handled hoe if Reagan's supporters want their employees to use it."

Soon, I received another call from the Board's secretary. The Board had set dates for public hearings for El Centro and Salinas.

On May 1, 1973, the Board held a hearing in the Imperial Valley. After Dr. Robert Murphy, an authority on lumbar disc disorders at the University of California at San Diego, explained the danger to farm workers that the short-handled hoe posed, Board member Turner asked, "Doctor, it seems to me that the thrust of what you are saying in its entirety is that the position that one has to assume in order to use the short hoe accelerates the wear and tear that would otherwise take place, and eventually results in pain or structural damage to the back because of accumulated stress. Is that the thrust of what you are saying?"

Dr. Murphy responded, "The thrust . . . is that the back tends to disintegrate anyway in everybody, and anybody who is a farm laborer, even if he uses a long hoe standing straight up, will have a certain degree of progressive change in his back which is normal. But what I'm saying is that the short hoe tremendously increases the rate [such] that the patient loses many years of productivity that he would otherwise not have to lose if he could use a hoe while standing up."

Board member Turner then stated, "You're saying then that perhaps the thirty-year-old guy that's in this kind of work [has a] sixty-year-old back."

Murphy affirmed the remark.

Doctor Murphy was followed by Dr. Robert Thompson, who specialized in treating farm workers. He testified as follows:

> The most common significant complaint is that of backaches, or chronic back strain, or back pain. I say significant because it's the one that really does contribute to any form of disability, which has already been emphasized. I just want to relate to you some of the comments that I frequently encounter in seeing patients. For example, my patients frequently do not complain about pain when they come to see me: "Yes, it hurts sometimes, maybe not right now, but it has hurt in the past and has bothered me." I have the feeling that they sort of expect this, that this is their way of life to have backaches, so records on how often farm workers complain of a specific back injury may be misleading. Another common comment that they make is, "No, my back doesn't bother me unless I work stooped over." And the most common reason that they do work stooped over is to use the short-handled hoe that they call the *cortito*. Another comment that I have heard at least on several occasions is that they would rather do any sort of work in the fields other than use the short-handled hoe.

Also in El Centro, the Board heard from an Imperial Valley neurosurgeon, Dr. Travis Calvin. He was in full agreement with Dr. Flanagan that the short hoe caused farm workers to suffer serious back problems.

At the El Centro hearing, Glick showed why a good attorney is so important. Like a toreador slowly wearing down his opponent, Glick presented witness after witness supporting our request that the Board ban the short-handled hoe. But the growers also presented evidence.

Following Doctors Murphy, Thompson, and Calvin, a grower's witness told the Board if he could not use the hoe he currently uses, he would be forced to switch to mechanization and massive herbicide spraying. He said that the crops grown in the Imperial and Salinas Valleys could not be thinned and weeded with any other tool, and he would no longer need workers to weed the fields. That would mean a loss of hundreds of thousands of jobs.

Imperial County lettuce grower Hector De la Vega told the Board, "It is absolutely impossible to thin lettuce that's planted in raw seed with a long-handled hoe. . . . Now, the industry has gone far ahead in precision seeding and things of that nature, but it hasn't completely been perfected, and especially in the Imperial Valley, where it's absolutely impossible to stand in our extreme summer temperatures, even if we did go to precision planting. So therefore it's my personal opinion that it's impossible to outlaw the short-handled hoe."

Lloyd Hegar testified, "I feel it [the short hoe] is very necessary to achieve the high yields and to achieve economic profits from the crops."

Otis Glendenning told the Board, "The reason the Imperial Valley uses the short-handled hoe, where some other areas do not, is because here agriculture is much more intensive."

Richard Hubbard testified, "If we spend more time by means of a long-handled hoe, or by a mechanical thinner, our prices go up and the price to the consumer is higher."

The next day, Eliseo Hernández told the Board he was sixty-five years old. He fought eighty-three fights as an amateur until 1928 and for the next five years fought some seventy-five fights as a professional. He quit fighting because of the Depression. He told the Board he was in good shape when a contractor took him up near Salinas to thin beets:

> The first two days, my body got pretty sore, and I thought my sores would go away because I had not been active for quite a few

days, but instead they began to get worse. At the end of a week, my body was pretty sore, especially my lower back. In the second week, it was harder on me. I could hardly take the pain in my back and legs. On the third week, it was just plain torture. It was very painful to keep on working. The men wanted to keep me on working and I said no. And I quit. And I swore and I vowed if I ever heard in the future a chance to hit that short hoe, I would hit it as hard as I possibly could. And I have waited thirty-nine years for a hearing on this short hoe. . . . After I quit thinning, I got paid and went into town. It was three weeks after that before I could straighten up without feeling no pain in my back. It was months and months before my pain really disappeared from my back.

Glick patiently tried to analyze the thoughts of the five conservative male elders who sat as Board members hearing testimony from farm workers and agribusiness-industry personnel. He felt good after seeing Board members' expressions when, following the hearing, Hernández was asked by the gubernatorial appointees why he was holding a golf club. Hernández responded that he used to work on the golf links and had meant to ask the Board how golfers could swing that long club and hit a tiny white ball, but farm workers could not take short swings with a long-handled hoe and hit weeds.

Two days later, in Salinas, the testimony began with a group of workers presented by Richard Thornton of the Growers-Shippers Association. Uniformly, they testified that the short hoe did not cause pain; in fact, they liked it. Typical was Lupe Ruiz who told the Board, "We've been doing lettuce for a long time and it doesn't bother my back or anything. You just go home and take a shower, and that's all."

The testifying for the growers' workers was followed by Hisauro Garza, a former farm worker, who told the Board the following:

I recall during the break in the afternoon about three or four o'clock that everybody would eagerly await this ten-minute break, would throw down the short-handled hoe, and with their bodies slightly bent forward from the excruciating pain and the bent position all day long, would try to roll over the rows where the vegetables, the lettuce or what have you was planted, to try to let the heat from the ground sort of massage their backs, and try to in that way sort of alleviate the pain.

He told the Board he would come home in dire pain and see his cousins "with small frames, ninety-five and hundred pounders, trying to lay back on their beds, and as their bodies kind of unfolded back to meet the bed surface, I could see the tears falling out of their eyes just crying from the pain."

Next came Robert Granger, associated with Eckel Produce. Apparently not having talked with the witnesses presented by the Growers-Shippers Association, he admitted that using the short hoe hurts badly for four or five days and then you get used to it, but it aches again if you take a day or two off. He told the Board that growers did not require use of the short hoe "just because we want to hurt somebody's back. It's a necessity."

Mervyn Bailey with Harden Farms told the Board, "My father ran a crew of Hindus in 1911 in the Salinas Valley in thinning and hoeing beets. Then Japanese. Then we followed with the Philippinos. And then the Mexicans. The stoop labor, most of them are small or more agile to handle it than the ordinary Anglo due to their build."

Unable to hide his outrage, Richard Chávez, César's brother told the Board that he was bothered by the comments on the stature of Mexicans. "If he's [the Mexican's] a shorter person," Richard said, "it's obvious he can stoop and it won't bother him. In other words, strong back, weak mind."

The Board heard from Manuel Olivas, who had been ranch manager for a farm worker cooperative Dave Kirkpatrick helped create. The intent of the cooperative was for members to reap a profit doing what they did best, farm work. In addition to acreage growing strawberries in Watsonville, the co-op grew row crops in the Salinas Valley. Olivas testified that some co-op members balked at having to use the short-handled hoe to thin lettuce. The members decided to allow members to use the hoe they chose to use. Some chose the short hoe and some the long hoe. According to Olivas:

In the beginning, for the ones that had never used the long-handled hoe, it was kind of awkward and clumsy, and it took them some time to get used to it. It took about a day and a half, I think; however, the short-handled hoe individuals were really getting it on. I mean, they were just, psttttt, right on down those rows, and they were laughing at the guys using the long-handled hoes, saying, ah, you're wasting your time. Late in the afternoon, the guys that had been yelling about, yeah, let's use the short-handled hoe, were on their knees. As any one of these individuals can testify that have come up before the commission, around the afternoon you take a drive up to the Salinas fields, and you'll find out how many people are running around on their knees. It is hard.

By the end of [the first] week, the individuals with the long-handled hoe were just as good as the ones with the short-handled hoe. Granted you still have doubles to pull off and you still have to bend over to get those doubles, but what you do have is a fresher individual by the end of the afternoon. You have a better quality of work done than by the guy with the short-handled hoe. The guy with the short-handled hoe was so tired, this thing gets so heavy, that after a while you're just going on the gravitational pull of the hoe itself. You're just letting it drop and it's coming down . . . I'm sure, if you kind of follow these individuals that are doing the thing, in the afternoon you'll find that they're a little bit more sloppy than they were in the morning, and they tend to leave bigger gaps between the lettuces which causes less yield production. You're supposed to leave it eight to twelve inches long. If you mess up and cut off the twelve-inch line, you've got twenty-four. That means you've lost one head of lettuce. You continue to do this and eventually it adds up.

After lunch, Dr. John Radebaugh, a San Joaquin Valley physician who was a member of the National Farm Workers Health group, testified. According to Radebaugh:

The prolonged strain in this unnatural attitude for the spine, especially for young people, is separation of the cartilages at a time when these cartilages are still in the developing stage. For older workers the strain over a long period of time produces stretching of the normal ligaments, instability of the back, and finally erosion of the cartilages of the bone, damage which is permanent and which may occur at a young age. How can this be prevented? By allowing work to be done in a more erect position as much as possible.

Using a model of the human spine, Doctor Radebaugh showed the Board how the stooped position compelled by use of the *cortito* caused painful disc damage. "In your commission," he told the Board, "you are looking for ways to prevent disease. I think one of the ways you can contribute most to the health of the farm worker at this point is to abolish the use of the short-handled hoe."

After discussing the use of the long-handled hoe elsewhere in the United States, Dr. Radebaugh summarized, ". . . with the observation that workers in California with whom I've had experience show considerably more back problems than those I noted in the East; I believe that this is directly due to the prevalent usage of the short hoe in California."

Before the hearings were over, the Board heard from eleven physicians who either specialized in back problems or had extensive experience treating farm workers. All eleven agreed that the use of the short-handled hoe over a substantial period of time caused abnormal degeneration of the spine, resulting in irreparable back injury and permanent disability. In the Imperial Valley, Dr. Robert Murphy expressed the essence of the unanimous medical testimony in the following terms:

> Maintaining the body in a bent position, as is necessary when using the short hoe, places great stress on the intervertebral discs of the spine, which accelerates the development of degenerative diseases of the spine, which occur secondary to the disc degeneration. As the disc degenerates it can no longer tolerate this stress. The stress is transmitted to the bones and to the other joints, which is the disease that we call arthritis. The

degeneration occurs in the joints and the bones as well as the intervertebral discs. Performance of simple activities while in the bent position adds further stresses, which are multiplied many times over what they would be in an erect position. The result of this is a worker whose spine ages more rapidly than the rest of his body until a point is reached where he is no longer able to work because of low back pain.

It should also be noted that none of the doctors who testified at the hearings on the short-handled hoe asked for or received any compensation for their testimony.

Finally, the hearings ended. The Board took the matter under submission. Based on the evidence we presented and the Board's attitude and questions by the time the hearings had finished in Salinas, Glick believed we had won.

Years later we were told that after the Salinas hearings had concluded, without telling or inviting us, growers presented the Board members with a private demonstration of use of the hoe during a complimentary dinner, enabling the agribusiness industry in our absence to apply strong pressure and insist that banning the short-handled hoe would ruin agriculture in California.

Naively, back in Salinas, I returned to the work I'd been doing for the past five years—helping California's rural poor deal with the problems of their daily life.

Twenty-four

ON JULY 13, 1973, after several months of fighting giants, like the knight errant Don Quixote, and seeing hundreds of clients after the Industrial Safety Board hearing, I returned from lunch to find a message to call Marty Glick.

"Are you ready to hear the decision in the short-handled hoe case?" Marty asked.

Suddenly the heart of my dream life was being pierced by reality, a decision from the Industrial Safety Board. Panic tightened my abdomen. "Do we have one?"

"An oral decision," said Glick, with ice in his usually warm and caring tone. "I wrote down word for word what the Board representative said. 'The Board denies the petition to prohibit further use of the short-handled hoe. The hoe is not an unsafe hand tool and the cost in discarding hundreds of thousands of hoes outweighs the harm resulting from their use.'"

"Oh, man," I moaned. "Discarding hoes outweighs the harm to hundreds of thousands of permanently disabled farm workers? The Board responsible for workers' safety is more worried about discarding old hoes than crippling workers. How can it say the short hoe is not an unsafe tool when all the medical evidence is to the contrary?"

"I'm stunned," Marty sighed. "It didn't give any reasons. I guess we can ask for a rehearing but I wouldn't bet on the result."

That afternoon, I called the Board to request a specific reason for the denial. The representative said that a memo was being drafted, but she would not tell me its contents. I knew I could ask for a rehearing within twenty days. To request a rehearing, I had to know the reasons the Board relied on to deny our petition. If the denial was merely another effort to preserve the power of the corporations over the people, as Marty and I suspected, we could show the reasons were frivolous in a petition with the court. I wrote the Board to confirm my oral request for reasons. I could wait a while, but not too long.

I waited until the nineteenth day. The reasons did not come. Finally, on August 3, I blindly filed the petition asking for a rehearing. The same day I received a letter from the director of the Industrial Relations Department. It stated as follows:

> Your recent letter inquires as to the Board's reasons for denying the farm workers' petition to prohibit use of the short-handled hoe.
>
> I am unable to supply all the reasons that each Board member may have had, but am able to pass along some of the ideas and thoughts brought up by individual members in conjunction with our public hearings and field visits. The following list includes in rough form some of these thoughts and individual conclusions:
>
> 1. Testimony failed to prove the tool unsafe.
> 2. Some workers have been found quite resistant to back deterioration even after many years of short-hoe usage.
> 3. Safety orders are not ideally suited to control of body deterioration problems, in part because any acceptable regulations would require built-in exceptions to adjust for wide variations in individual susceptibility to damage.
> 4. Back deterioration is a widespread problem associated with so many activities and operations, both on and off the job, that effective control depends mainly upon far-reaching changes in established attitudes and modes of living.

The Industrial Safety Board denied our request for a rehearing.

The following day I went to San Francisco to talk with Glick about our next step. We walked to a coffee shop around the corner from the tiny CRLA central office on Market Street. While we sat at a Formica table waiting for our cheeseburgers and Cokes, Glick smiled.

"Cheer up, Jourdane," he urged. "If you would have listened to what I was saying from the start, you would have expected this."

"I'm just pissed we wasted so much time going through their hearings."

"I think they call that due process."

"We'll sue the growers in court one by one and go through a thousand trials if that's what it takes to stop the torture to stooped farm workers."

"Why are we going to sue each grower individually?"

"To get real due process, to prove the short hoe is an unsafe hand tool."

Glick smiled. "Mo, we can just sue the Industrial Safety Board and ask the court to order it to enforce the law."

Glick reminded me that a year earlier I had sued the state welfare department and made it enforce a law requiring it to provide child care to mothers who could work and get off welfare if they had child care.

"This is the same," he maintained.

I grinned. "Marty, you're so smart. No wonder you're the main boss here in San Francisco and I'm a lowly staff attorney in Salinas."

Glick laughed. "I'd trade with you in a minute. You're still seeing clients. I spend all my time fighting to keep the federal government from accepting Reagan's claim that we're a waste of taxpayers' money and that you should spend more time doing paperwork and less time representing the poor, most of whom Reagan's people apparently believe are unworthy of representation with taxpayers' money."

Since we were raising an issue of statewide interest in *Carmona v. Industrial Safety Board*, we could seek an original writ in the Supreme Court. In terms regular people understand, that meant we could request that the Supreme Court ban the short-handled hoe as a dangerous tool without first making the request in a lower court. Again, we prepared a petition with attached affidavits, including Sebastián Carmona telling the court:

> I first came to the United States in 1950 and worked in the fields around Santa Rosa, Texas. From 1950 to 1959, I experienced all phases of agriculture from planting to harvesting lettuce, tomatoes, cabbage, sugar beets, okra, and parsley, all with

a long-handled hoe. I later migrated to Soledad, California in 1959, and started working for Salinas Strawberries as a foreman. I found myself obligated to make my people use short-handled hoes. They told me I could accept things the way they were or lose my job.

Glick and I knew we had to convince the court that the human back could not withstand the strain of constant stooping. Dr. David Flanagan, recounting his testimony before the State Industrial Safety Board, told the Supreme Court:

> The ligaments (of the lower back) become stretched, scarred, and lax. The joints become ragged, irregular, and denuded of the smooth articulate surfaces. The discs (cushioning pads between the vertebrae) become brittle with cracks and seepage of the liquid centers, which then bulge and apply pressure on the nearby nerves to the lower extremities. The bones fracture in some cases, and these fractures do not heal.

We spent the weekend preparing the doctors' affidavits just as we had a year before when we filed our petition with the state Board; and we built our case largely on the bodies of evidence assembled during the Board review process: the survey showing the high incidence of back injuries among farm workers who used the short-handled hoe, proof that the long hoe was used elsewhere to do the same work done in California with the short hoe, and transcripts of the testimony presented at the Industrial Safety Board hearings. On October 11, 1973, we walked to the Supreme Court and filed our petition.

Eight Salinas Valley farm workers, Sebastián Carmona, Isabel Cardena, Ramundo Daniel, Eligio de Haro, Emilio García, Juan López, José Romero, and Jesús Serrano, representing a class of thousands of other farm workers, told the California Supreme Court that their employers compelled them to work in a stooped position with their heads at or below waist level for eight to twelve hours a day. They told the court they were forced to work in this abnormal position because their employers required them to use a hoe with a handle approximately a foot in length rather than a hoe with a normal handle.

The abnormal position caused them to suffer severe pain and ultimately resulted in permanent disabling back injuries. They told the court about filing the petition with the Industrial Safety Board, the Board's hearings, the testimony by farm workers that use of the short hoe caused severe pain, and the unanimous testimony by physicians that use of the short-handled hoe caused permanent back injury. They told the court about the Board's summary rejection of their petition for relief and the letter the Board finally wrote in response to their request for reasons. The farm workers begged the court to see that substantial evidence did not support the Board's determination.

Twenty-five

ARRIVING IN SALINAS two days after filing the petition in the Supreme Court, I shuffled through the stack of waiting mail on my desk. I shivered when I saw an envelope from the Supreme Court. I tore it open. My excitement plunged when I read an order dated October 12, 1973, "The petition in *Carmona v. Industrial Safety Board* is transferred to the Court of Appeals, First District."

I called Glick. He told me all that the transfer meant was that the Supreme Court wanted the lower court to have a chance to consider the issue before it did. All we could do was wait and see what the court of appeals decided.

"But it also means it took the Supreme Court one day to decide that the problem is not important enough for it to decide without our going through the lower courts first, right?" I asked.

"If you look at it that way, I think we're in trouble, Jourdane," Glick admitted. "Just be glad the court didn't summarily dismiss our petition. We'd be out of court with no place to go, but I've always told you we can win in the end. We just can't give up."

Twenty-six

SIX MONTHS LATER, after the Supreme Court transferred sixteen short-handled hoe cases to the court of appeals, a three-judge panel in San Francisco summarily denied our petition. I called Glick. The more senior lawyer counseled me, "I understand why you think it's unfair, Jourdane. Sometimes it doesn't seem like you're getting your day in court when they deny your petition without allowing you to tell them in person why you're right. But that's the way courts are. Thank God, we still have the Supreme Court."

"Do you think we have a chance there?" I asked desperately.

"Rarely will any court reverse a Safety Board's decision. Normally, courts affirm whatever an administrative agency does, if there's what they call substantial evidence supporting the Board decision. Court's say the agency has substantial evidence if there is almost any evidence supporting the decision. But the decision here is so outrageous in light of the evidence that I think we have a chance."

Glick and I remained at the office until the middle of the night. The next day, May 23, 1974, we filed with the state high court our petition for a rehearing. We included affidavits of farm workers and doctors, the survey showing the high incidence of back injuries among farm workers who used the short-handled hoe, evidence the long hoe was used elsewhere to do the same work done in California with the short hoe, and transcripts of the testimony presented at the Industrial Safety Board hearings.

Twenty-seven

LOOKING AT MY MAIL on May 30, 1974, I discovered an order of the Supreme Court issued on May 28:

Petition for hearing granted and cause transferred to this court.

Let a writ of review issue, to be heard before this court when the proceeding is ordered on calendar.

The writ is to be issued, served and filed on or before May 29, 1974.

The written return to the writ is to be served and filed on or before June 14, 1974.

I called Glick.

"Marty, this means we have a chance," I said. "For the first time since we started this case, I feel optimistic about our chances. What happens now? I mean do we have to do anything?"

"Well, the court will probably set the short-hoe case for oral argument. At oral argument we and the growers' lawyers will argue the merits of the case. We'll be asked questions the court has about the petition. We've come a long way with an impossible case, Mo. Since the court granted the writ of review, I think it'll reverse the Industrial Safety Board decision, especially since all the evidence supports the farm workers. If we can get the court to outlaw the hoe, we win. But usually when the Supreme Court concludes that a lower court or agency like the Industrial Safety Board has misinterpreted the law, it will reverse the decision and remand and give the lower court or agency another chance to decide the case. If it remands, we may be starting all over with the hearings. Even worse, the court might be granting oral argument just to avoid bad press. Both the *Los Angeles Times* and the *San Francisco Chronicle* have been writing good articles about your petition. Plus public television in LA had a good documentary on what we're doing."

On July 24, 1994, Bud Antle, Inc. filed an amicus curiae or friend of the court brief with the Supreme Court. The world's largest lettuce grower attempted to have us thrown out of court without the court considering the merits of the farm workers' claim. The company's lawyers argued the Industrial Safety Board's decision was not reviewable by a court because it was a reasonable "quasi-legislative" determination of a state agency charged by California lawmakers to interpret worker safety violations. Negating the Board's decision under these circumstances, Bud Antle argued, would risk imposing new legal rights and remedies beyond those intended by the legislature. Bud Antle also argued the record did not show the short-handled hoe was unsafe; and that the short hoe should not be prohibited, because it was necessary (or at least economically advantageous) for agriculture to require its use.

We responded with a thirty-three-page brief.

We reminded the high court that the farm workers were only seeking enforcement of existing laws. Labor Code sections 6400 and 6401 required employers to maintain practices which were reasonably adequate to render employment safe. Section 6500 gave the Division of Industrial Safety authority to further the statutes. Pursuant to that authority, it adopted section 3316, or Title 8 of the Administrative Code, that prohibited employers from forcing employees to use unsafe hand tools. Labor Code section 142 required the Division to enforce safety orders. In their petition, the farm workers concluded with a prayer that the Division of Industrial Safety "enforce sections 3316 of Title 8" and "prohibit the use" of an unsafe hand tool commonly known as the short-handled hoe. We reminded the court that no new legislation was being sought, merely enforcement of an existing safety order.

Regarding Bud Antle's claim that the short-handled hoe had not been shown unsafe, we reminded the court that the Division of Industrial Safety had heard from eleven physicians, all of whom concluded that use of the short-handled hoe caused permanent disability; there was no medical evidence to the contrary.

Marty Glick's earlier prophecy, that the case could turn on proving the short hoe was not necessary to perform the work in the fields, proved correct when we considered Bud Antle's third contention: that the *cortito* was logistically and economically necessary for agriculture to require its use. Making the contention, Bud Antle relied on Labor Code section 6306, subdivision (a), which provided in relevant part that "Safe, safety, and health," as applied to employment or a place of employment, means such freedom from danger to the life, safety, or health of employees as the nature of the employment reasonably permits."

In our response, we began by saying that Bud Antle was misreading the term "nature of the employment reasonably permits." We agreed that some jobs, such as being a stunt flyer or crop duster are inherently hazardous. To make them safe would require banning the employment. We asked the court to recognize that weeding with a hoe is not, per se, hazardous since an alternative to bending over, use of the long-handled hoe, is used to perform the job throughout the United States. It is the tool that is hazardous or unsafe, not the nature of the employment.

Regarding Bud Antle's claim that it would be economically harmful to thin and weed with the long-handled hoe, we reminded the court that the owner and operator of Hubbard Farms testified that he usually sought a yield of around 24,000 heads of lettuce per acre at a cost of between $500 and $525 per acre. Thus, the cost to produce lettuce was around 2.1 cents per head. The price paid to the grower for lettuce in 1973 in Salinas ranged from 7.4 to 12.9 cents per head. Even if thinning and weeding with a long hoe to save the farm workers' backs were slower and the cost of thinning and weeding the crops increased, the slight increase in cost would be *de minimus* compared to the corporations' profits and the cost to the worker and to society as a whole when a farm worker became disabled.

Twenty-eight

SEVERAL MONTHS LATER, with Glick and other San Francisco attorneys acting as the justices, I practiced arguing the short-hoe case. By the time of the real argument in the Supreme Court a few days later, I was ready. The justices did not ask me any questions that Marty and his associates had not asked in the mock hearing. I left the courtroom feeling the high court would reverse the Industrial Safety Board decision, but I had no idea whether they would ban the use of the short-handled hoe based on the evidence we presented before the Industrial Safety Board or remand to enable the Board to reconsider whether farm workers should be required to continue destroying their backs with the tool known as *El brazo del diablo,* or "the Devil's Arm."

Walking into the Salinas office on a Wednesday morning in January, 1975, I leafed through the mail. Seeing the envelope dated January 13 from the California Supreme Court, I knew I was about to see a decision in *Carmona v. Industrial Safety Board.* I looked at the last line of the opinion. "Petition granted."

"We won," I shouted. "We won the short-handled hoe case."

Within seconds, the entire staff was in my office. I read the five-page opinion aloud. It ended, "In sum, we conclude that the respondent agency erred in determining that it would be an unreasonable extension of its authority to find that the short-handled hoe is an unsafe hand tool."

"I can't believe we won on that crazy legal theory," I laughed to Glick over the phone.

"Mo. We haven't won, yet. The Supreme Court says the Industrial Safety Board was wrong in denying our petition, but the court sent the case back to the Board to try again."

"With the evidence we presented to the Industrial Safety Board, and (liberal) Jerry Brown now serving as governor,[1] how can we lose?"

"You're probably right, but even when the short hoe is outlawed, we didn't win this case. The farm workers won it. We just told their story to the court. When people are suffering as much as the workers have been with the short hoe, you don't need much law to have a court of honest men like our Supreme Court say we will not permit the injustice to continue. All it took was a little persistence on our part to get someone to listen to what the farm workers were saying."

During the spring of 1975, the Board held renewed hearings on the short-handled hoe in San Diego and Salinas. In San Diego, the Ybarra family, Minnie and her sons Richard and Danny, gathered a group of neighbors to testify. Farm worker after farm worker told of the pain and disability and begged the Board to stop growers from forcing them to use the short hoe. Over and over, like parrots trained by the same lawyer, corporate growers told the Board that use of the short-handled hoe did not cause injury to the farm workers. Richard Maltzman, a San Francisco attorney representing Bud Antle, Inc., the large lettuce grower that got César Chávez jailed in 1970 for refusing to stop farm workers from engaging in a nonviolent boycott and that argued against the farm workers' effort to ban the short-handled hoe in the Supreme Court, presented the Board with a Palo Alto doctor's statement saying that perhaps the high incidence of back problems among Mexican farm workers was because of a genetic deficiency. He told of a group of Eskimos who also had a high degree of back disease.

During a break in a morning recess in the San Diego hearing, when a community worker and I were standing in the hallway talking, a six-foot, 220-pound man stepped between the petite community worker and me.

"Who the fuck do you think you are?" stormed the fortyish Coachella Valley grower, pushing me in the chest. "You think you can come into our valley and tell us how to farm?" Again he pushed me, knocking me into the wall.

---

[1]Democrat Edmund G. ("Jerry") Brown, Jr. was elected to succeed Ronald W. Reagan as California's governor in November 1974.

Suddenly, the large man was surrounded by scrappy small farm workers who rushed over to save their attorney. Three company supervisors, seeing their boss in trouble, ran down the hall to save him. Just as a free-for-all was about to erupt, state police officers raced down the hallway.

That afternoon, Imperial Valley lettuce grower Jack Flemming told the Board, "I have a $20,000 electrical thinner. I never use it because there is no doubt that farm workers can do a better job by hand. If you abolish the short-handled hoe, I am going to go out and crank up that electrical thinner."

Two days later when hearings resumed in Salinas, I had a chance to respond to what the Board had heard in San Diego. On March 27, 1975, I told the Board the following:

> Until Monday of this week, it was undisputed that stooping to use the short hoe causes back injury to the farm workers. The division has heard from eleven doctors, all of whom were either specialists in those problems or had extensive experience in treating farm workers. The testimony of those doctors unanimously supported the following conclusions: 1. Use of the short-handled hoe causes abnormal degeneration of the spine resulting in irreparable and permanent disability. 2. Their testimony supports the conclusion that this type of injury is rarely remediable, and finally that the posture required when using the short-handled hoe causes severe pain to the farm workers who have to use it. Now, as I said, until Monday there was no contrary evidence. On Monday, you will recall, Mr. Maltzman, the attorney for Bud Antle, Inc., contended that the medical evidence which had been presented was deficient and he said that what the doctors did was jump a gap to look at the large number of back injuries that farm workers who use the short-handled hoe have and they jumped to the conclusion that these injuries were caused by the short-handled hoe. Well, I would say look at the record. That is not the case. The doctors described at length and in detail exactly how the injury occurs and exactly the type of injury that occurs. [. . .] Now the Board is told that not only can Mexican workers do

stoop labor because of their racial makeup, but they also have a higher incidence of back faults, apparently because they and the Eskimos evolved from the same stock.

Richard Thornton, vice-president of the Salinas Valley Growers-Shippers, testified next and told the Board it would be economically disastrous for it to ban the short-handled hoe. "Without the short-handled hoe there is no other tool at the present time to get a proper stand of the crop. We know agriculture is hard, hot, laborious work. But if we outlaw the short-handled hoe, what's next?" Thornton said he felt the entire issue of stoop labor was on trial.

Lettuce grower Tom Merrill testified, "Unless we're able to weed that crop with the short-handled hoe, we are going to have to disk the crop up. It will cost a fortune if we are stopped from using the short-handled hoe. If you ban this tool, through your hasty action, you will bankrupt California's largest industry."

Finally, the Board again took the matter under submission.

Twenty-nine

SINCE WE BEGAN THE SHORT-HANDLED HOE CASE, Governor Jerry Brown, who believed strongly in improving the lives of farm workers, had replaced Governor Ronald Reagan, who saw it as un-American to interfere with how agribusiness corporations treated their employees. Governor Brown appointed Don Vial, an old union man, to be the director of the Department of Industrial Welfare that oversaw the work of the Industrial Safety Board. But Vial worked under Rose Bird, Governor Brown's Secretary of Business and Transportation. This left Marty Glick and me skeptical after we spoke with her about the short-handled hoe in Sacramento. Over the following months, a period of time that seemed to me like years, the governor appointed Marty to the position of Director of California's Employment Development Department, one of the largest departments in the state. Marty and Steve Ibarra talked with Mario Obledo, the former director of the Mexican-American Legal Defense and Educational Fund (MALDEF) and with one of Bob Gnaizda's co-founders of Public Advocates, Tony Kline. Governor Brown had appointed Obledo to the post of Secretary of Health and Human Services and Kline to Secretary of Legal Affairs. But it was not until César Chávez spoke with the governor on April 7, 1995, that Rose Bird announced that the short-handled hoe was an unsafe hand tool.

On April 17, 1975, the Salinas *Californian* reported that the state had banned the short-handled hoe. Not surprisingly, the ban drew a pleased reaction from the farm workers and anger from the growers. In the article, the *Californian* reported that I was pleased the Supreme Court and the governor believed the workers instead of the corporations, as the government historically had done. Richard Thornton, direc-

The Long-Handled Hoe

Five years after Sebastián Carmona told Mo Jourdane about his back injury, the California Supreme Court found the *cortito* caused farm workers to become crippled for life, and Governor Brown banned the tool from California fields. (Courtesy of *The Sacramento Bee*, Dennis Renault, 1975) tor of the has-been Growers-Shippers Vegetable Association, said the decision to ban the short hoe would severely and harshly impact Salinas Valley agriculture.

That night, California Rural Legal Assistance staff and hundreds of Salinas Valley farm workers drank beer in the Ven a Mexico Cantina in Soledad. Around midnight, I walked from the bar toward my car. While I proceeded slowly, my head down, a slender farm worker in his late forties caught up with me. The older worker placed his hands on my shoulders and embraced me. Tears running down his cheek, he managed to say, "Thank you, *Abogado*. It has been a very long fight. I thank God that when you saw us bent over in the field, you could not walk away. The only way I can pay you is with my prayers and this." Standing proudly, the graying worker handed me his short-handled hoe. "Thanks to you, I do not need this any more."

On April 9, 1975, in an editorial "An End to the Crippling," the *Los Angeles Times* pointed out that the medical evidence had always been indisputable. The short-handled hoe caused spinal injury that crippled farm workers. The *Times* noted that it took a unanimous Supreme Court decision and a clear mandate by the governor to get the barbarous tool out of California's fields.

The *Fresno Bee* editorial "Short Hoe Must Go" on January 15, 1975 said, "It took determined legal advocacy and prodding by the California Supreme Court, but at last the state has banned the use of the short-handled hoe." The *Fresno Bee* recognized the medical testimony that the short hoe was inherently unsafe "was irrefutable." The *Bee* added, "Some growers' groups, particularly those in the Salinas Valley, say switching to . . . alternatives [like the long-handled hoe] will cause problems and increase costs," but concluded, "No economic structure should be subsidized by human suffering."

The same day, the *Modesto Bee* reported that the Western Growers Association, representing around 80 percent of the row-crop growers in California and Arizona, wanted a delay in enforcement of the ban. From his Newport Beach office, Daryl Arnold, the association's vice-president, said the delay was necessary "for answers to what if a worker prefers a short handle or what if a handle breaks." Richard Thornton told the Salinas *Californian* that the growers' first step would probably be litigation in the courts, asking for a delay of the banning. Then the growers would seek relief under the Occupational Safety and Health Act.

The next day, the *Brawley News* reported that attorneys for the Western Growers Association were seeking a restraining order in Orange County Superior Court. The *News* reported that, in any case, it did not appear as though the state was enforcing the ban. The paper said that El Centro Imperial Store manager, Robert Tuttle, reported a number of long-handled hoes had been sold the day after the short hoe was banned, but soon the sales were canceled apparently because growers realized that the ban was not being enforced. Again, no one was policing the fields for violation of the law that protected farm workers.

The same day, the *Watsonville Register-Pajaronian* reported that the Western Growers Association's attorneys claimed the Division of Industrial Safety did not have legal authority to ban the short-handled hoe.

AG ALERT, the California Farm Bureau Federation publication, warned its readers that if the ban on the use of the short hoe was allowed to stand, it would have massive effects on the harvesting and thinning of vegetables.

Three days later, on April 14, the Orange County court held a hearing on the growers' request for a temporary stay of the ban. Donald Dresser appeared for the Western Growers, and I appeared for the workers. The court denied the request for a stay and set a May hearing on the merits of the growers' claims.

The same day, ironically, Bud Antle, Inc., the world's largest grower-shipper operation, the corporation that had bitterly opposed banning the short-handled hoe, reported that the switch to the long-handled hoe was not only "not a problem," but had markedly increased production in the field. Antle said its crews adjusted quickly to the long-handled hoe and that, as a result, production had increased 5 to 10 percent. The *Sacramento Bee* was astonished that employers did not already know this. The paper noted that farm workers, including César Chávez, who himself had an injured back caused by the short-handled hoe, had been protesting use of the short-handled hoe for years and had been insisting that the length of a hoe's handle would make little difference in the field but would have an immense effect on farm workers' health.

Before the Orange County court ruled on the merits of the growers' request, the San Diego office of the State Division of Industrial Safety gave variances to four Imperial Valley growers: Gourmet Food, Collace Brothers, LeBrucherie Ranches, and Jackson Farming. The San Diego office of the Division of Industrial Safety was accepting at face value the growers' claim that no long-handled hoes were available. Meanwhile, in the Salinas Valley, Grower-Shippers' spokesman Richard Thornton told the Salinas *Californian* that growers were "complying as rapidly as possible," but there had been difficulty obtaining long-handled hoes. He claimed that even stores in San Jose, sixty miles to the north, had no more long-handled hoes in stock. The *Californian*'s own telephone check ended with one call. The reporter found Farmers Mercantile in Salinas had long-handled hoes on hand and expected more. The store manager said there appeared to be many long-handled hoes available.

The same day, Héctor de la Rosa told the reporter he had driven from Gonzalez to Salinas that morning and "saw the most wonderful thing in my life. Two or three crews using the long hoe."

As far away as New York, the *Times* saw through the growers' fantasy when it reported on May 10, 1975 that California lawyers appeared to have won all but the final battle in years of litigation over an occupational practice that endangered farm workers. The *Times* article reported that use of a hoe with a twelve-inch handle forced workers to stoop, causing "persistent back injury." The paper reported that California's growers had decided the short hoe was more efficient than the long-handled hoe used in other parts of the country because the workers could "get closer to the crops."

By mid-May most growers were reluctantly using the long-handled hoe, although many labor contractors continued to violate the law, and the Superior Court in Orange County had denied the Western Growers Association request that the lower court reverse the state's highest legal authority, the California Supreme Court.

Not long after the growers lost in Orange County, considered by many to be the most conservative county in the country, they carried out their earlier threat and sought relief before the federal Occupational Safety and Health Agency, an agency whose leadership had been appointed by the Nixon-Ford administrations. By then, I had left CRLA, but nevertheless testified as a witness at an OSHA hearing on the short-handled hoe held in the Imperial Valley. Again the growers lost. In the words reprinted in the *San Francisco Chronicle,* the *Sacramento Bee,* and the *Fresno Bee* on April 25, 1975, "Since the largest lettuce producer has found that the long-handled hoe gets more done in a day with less loss of stamina, other employers would appear to have no ground to stand on in offering further resistance to the ban on *el cortito.*"

Lester Hubbard of the Western Growers Association, however, still maintained that "Costs will go up and everyone will suffer financially."

César Chávez responded, "That is the way it works, you see. As long as the grower can produce his crops cheaply, it doesn't matter that he is destroying the workers. He says there is no other way. But when he is forced to change, the solutions appear like a miracle. That is the way it is with California agriculture."

Thirty

FOR A FEW MONTHS, I tried to talk with clients and work on cases in the Salinas office. Finally, I told Angie I was driving down to Soledad to talk with Héctor about personal things. In Soledad, Héctor and I went around the corner from the office to a pool hall, bought a pitcher of Michelob and racked a game of eight ball. I slowly slid the cue between my index finger and thumb, preparing to break the balls.

"I just need to do something different," I told Héctor.

"You've been working here for a long time, *compadre*. Why don't you take some time off and do something different for a while?"

"Maybe I will," I responded, watching the yellow one-ball fall into a corner pocket. I walked around the table to take aim on the orange five-ball.

"You know, a couple days ago I was talking with Gil Flores in Delano," Héctor said. "He told me the legislature just passed the Agricultural Labor Relations Act. It gives farm workers the right to vote in secret on whether they want to have a union. Maybe you should go to Sacramento and help the people get the new law started. Most people in government know very little about farm workers. The new law is real important."

Other than my work on the short-handled hoe case, I had no experience in labor law. When I met Marty Glick seven years earlier, I congratulated him for helping to get rid of the Bracero Program. Glick admitted he didn't always win. He told me he had just received an adverse decision in a case against Salinas Strawberry Company, which had fired farm workers because they supported a union. Glick told me, "Under established California law, farm workers have no right to support a union. But you don't have to worry about that. The federal government doesn't allow CRLA to get involved in union cases."

The evening after speaking with Héctor at the pool hall, I telephoned Gil. "I remember thinking you could never win the *cortito* case," he said, "but thank God I was wrong. I guess you'll probably quit representing farm workers now that you won the case that brought you into our struggle."

"I'm not sure what I'm gonna do. Today I heard about a new law for farm workers. You know anything about it?"

Gil told me that Governor Brown had gotten the legislature to pass it, and the growers were screaming. For the first time in history, farm workers would have the legal right to join a union. The new law would prohibit growers from interfering with that right.

Before hanging up, he said, "Mo, I know you could go to San Francisco or Los Angeles and make a lot of money, but don't abandon us. We need lawyers like you. It's good you stopped the companies from forcing us to work stooped over with the *cortito,* but you've been a lawyer for farm workers for almost ten years, so you know we have other big problems. The new law will give you a chance to really do something about those problems. Farm workers finally have the chance to choose whether they want to be in César's union or not. If you can make sure the elections are fair, you will be doing far more than you did by getting rid of the *cortito*."

Gil suggested I talk with some longtime Chávez supporters he knew. They could tell me about the history of the farm workers' fight.

Thirty-one

THE SATURDAY MORNING after I spoke with Gil, I drove to Arvin, a small town in the southeast corner of the San Joaquin Valley. Looking around, I saw a handful of scattered farm workers' houses clustered in a grape field. On one corner sat a Filipino store, across the street an elementary school, down the block a Catholic Church. I saw no traffic signals, no shopping mall, and almost no people.

I knocked on the door of a tiny wooden home and introduced myself to heavyset Elvira Guzmán who invited me in. "Lawyer," said the grandmotherly farm worker in Spanish, "these are my neighbors, Mr. and Mrs. Fuentes and Nora Tabárez."

I shook hands with the three dark farm workers sitting at the wooden kitchen table. "*Señores*," I slowly began in my less-than-perfect Spanish, but my words yielded to the aroma of Elvira Guzmán's high-mountain coffee when she set the steaming mug before me. Sipping the Central American gift, I continued, "As you know, the governor has just signed a law allowing farm workers to vote in secret on whether they want a union. I understand you can tell me what led to the new law."

The five sat in silence. Finally, Nora urged Elvira to begin, since it was her house.

"I work for Tejon Ranch," the elderly farm worker said in educated Spanish. Tejon is one of the largest grape growers in the Valley. Elvira said she met César Chávez when she was working for DiGiorgio Vineyards in 1965. That year, a group of Filipino workers in Delano left the rose field because the boss refused to give them water to drink. Chávez joined their struggle. "With César Chávez," Elvira boasted, "we at DiGiorgio went on strike. About 1,000 of us grape

134

pickers walked out."

Elvira continued in her clear Spanish. "We were part of workers striking across the Valley. We wanted more than the dollar-ten an hour they paid us to work from dawn to dusk in the dusty 110-degree fields. We wanted toilets in the fields so we wouldn't have to hold it all day with bad pains in our sides."

As Elvira spoke, the words came faster, her face became redder. "When we asked for a few cents an hour more and toilets, they laughed at us, called us wetbacks. They told us to go back to Mexico if we didn't like it here." Elvira told me she had lived in the same house for thirty years. Her children were born there. "I am American as much as those white growers. Pardon, Mr. Lawyer," she said proudly.

When Elvira paused, Nora interrupted. "Let me talk, *comadre*," she said, brushing her long, straight, black hair from her face. "You get so angry when you talk about how it was. I don't want you to have a *pinchi* heart attack. I might have just been a teenager but I was there, too."

Turning to me, Nora continued. "When the company threatened to fire us and hire workers from Mexico, we got scared and went back to work." She said they had babies to feed. They couldn't afford to lose their jobs. She said that for the next three years, the company rejected their pleas and prayers. They refused to recognize the United Farm Workers as their union.

Elvira interrupted, "But César Chávez led a successful grape boycott across the United States and Canada. The companies gave in."

"I think almost all the Delano companies which grow much of the country's grapes signed contracts with César," I said.

"*Sí*, and some lettuce companies in Salinas, like Interharvest, entered into contracts with César's union. For the first time, there were toilets in the fields," said Nora. "And for the first time, there was drinking water. For the first time, we got breaks. For the first time, we could file a grievance when a foreman touched my bottom or breast."

"Let me talk," demanded Elvira, obviously accustomed to leading. "After César fought so hard to get us better working conditions, the damn Teamsters decided they should be our union. They didn't care that we had no toilets and no water until César came. All they wanted was our dues."

Elvira said that she had heard that in the winter of 1970, the Teamster bosses attended a Farm Bureau Convention and agreed that the Teamsters and growers could help one another. If the companies signed contracts with the Teamsters, the Teamsters would collect millions in dues from the farm workers, and the growers could keep César Chávez out of their fields.

"So the companies signed with the Teamsters?" I asked rhetorically.

Elvira nodded. "No one asked us what we wanted. We lost almost everything Chávez had won for us."

"So you refused to work," I said.

"Over 3,600 farm workers were arrested, almost all for violating anti-picketing orders signed by judges in the little towns around here that the corporate growers control. Many of us were beaten. There were over fifty shootings. Some died."

"I remember hearing about workers being killed," I said.

"In August 1973?" asked Nora. "A young Yemeni immigrant interpreted for the United Farm Workers among his fellow grape workers. He was talking with some friends outside a restaurant in Lamont, when a sheriff hit him in the head with a five-cell flashlight. He had done nothing wrong. He died."

"Juan de la Cruz, too?" I asked.

"*Sí.* Juan was sixty years old. He was shot on a picket line near here. Like many farm workers, he first came to the United States as a bracero."

"And like many of us, he returned with his family and migrated from field to field until he found a good grower who respected his ability and hired him every year," said Elvira. "Juan worked at the same farm for many years before he was murdered."

"He was with the union since the start, wasn't he?" I asked.

"Yes, he joined the union in 1965," Elvira replied. He saw much improvement in the fields after César finally got the companies to talk with us. Then a young *pendejo* shot from the back of a pickup truck and took the strong union supporter's life."

"And a jury acquitted the killer, who said he just meant to shoot into the field," Nora added, speaking so fast I missed half of what she said. "But you're here to hear about how the law was passed, Mr. Lawyer, not just about the brave men and women who support César Chávez."

"Keep going," I said. "I'm learning. The *Los Angeles Times* said the new law passed because several thousand of you were on strike."

"And thousands of us in jail," said Nora, again speaking too rapidly for my limited understanding of Spanish. "They arrested me five times for, *cómo se dice*,[1] failure to disperse."

"*Perdón, señora,* I still have some trouble understanding Spanish. Can you speak a little slower?" I asked.

Nora smiled. Speaking slower, she resurrected events from an unforgettable past. "They arrested me on the picket line. The welfare department took my baby." Tears trickled down her smooth brown cheeks. "They took her for three weeks until Rural Legal Assistance helped me. Some mothers never got their babies back."

Mr. Fuentes finally spoke. "Teamster goons imported from Los Angeles were everywhere, but César would not let us fight the way unions did in the old days, even though the goons spit at us and pushed us around."

"Instead, César fasted," said Elvira, "and walked to Sacramento, three hundred miles to the north, with a couple hundred of us farm workers and priests. We went to ask our new young Governor Brown for help. By the time we entered the capital a month later, thousands of farm workers had joined us. You should have seen it. Right in front were little César Chávez and Delores Huerta carrying a brightly colored painting of the Virgin of Guadalupe."

"Like that one?" I asked, pointing to the wall above the sofa.

"Precisely," said Elvira. "The governor gave us hope. He promised us a law to protect our right to choose whether we wanted the Teamsters or César Chávez's union. The governor promised us we would receive a union wage and have toilets in the fields."

"And Governor Brown fulfilled his promise," I said.

"But will the new law be enforced?" Elvira asked.

---

[1]*Cómo se dice* is Spanish for "how do you say."

Thirty-two

EARLY IN AUGUST 1975, I started to work with the Farm Labor Board. When I arrived in the state capital late in the afternoon, I glanced at the digital thermometer outside the bank at Seventh and L Streets. It was 105 degrees. The next morning I walked into the new Agricultural Labor Relations Board's central office. I met the staff, the general counsel, the deputy general counsel, one secretary, and the only trial lawyer, Ron Greenberg.

Sitting in Burger King eating lunch with Greenberg on my first day, I studied the text of the new law. Under the recently enacted Agricultural Labor Relations Act, if a majority of workers on a farm signed cards requesting an election, within seven days they voted in secret for the union of their choice or no union. Farm workers could finally choose whether they wanted to be in César's union or not, and they could not be fired for supporting the union.

"I hope you have more experience in labor law than me," I admitted.

"Not much," responded Greenberg. "I worked at the National Labor Relations Board for a couple years right out of law school, but I've been doing criminal law in Berkeley for the past ten years."

"That's more than my zero experience," I replied.

"You'll learn fast. We have less than a month to prepare for the flood of threatened lawsuits intended to stop the Board before we hold the first election."

A few days later, the Agricultural Labor Board's general counsel hired a third lawyer, Byron Georgiou. Georgiou had grown up in Detroit, graduated *summa cum laude* from Stanford, and attended Harvard Law School. Georgiou confessed he had less experience with

'This year, Labor Day is beginning to mean something.'

Through the tireless effort of César Chávez, Dolores Huerta, Jerry Cohen, CRLA, and Governor Brown, in 1975 California outlawed the use of the short-handled hoe in the fields, passing the Agricultural Labor Relations Act that allowed farm workers to join and support the union of the choice, and provided them, for the first time, with a benefit that other laborers had received since the Great Depression: Unemployment Insurance. (Courtesy of *The Sacramento Bee*, Dennis Renault, 1975) labor law than Greenberg. During the year since he graduated from law school, he had clerked for Federal Judge Robert Peckham in San Francisco.

"We didn't have any cases dealing with labor law," he told us.

"But you probably learned a lot about writs and injunctions working with Peckham," I said.

"Not really. I came here with the understanding that of the three of us, you were the one with writ and injunction experience. We're going to need to make sure the new law is enforced."

When the Agricultural Labor Relations Act went into effect, Greenberg, Georgiou, and I were the full-time legal staff for the general counsel. We were weak in the field of law we were about to enter. Our only chance to level the playing field against the experienced labor law attorneys of the companies and Teamsters we would oppose was our readiness to work whatever hours were necessary to represent the farm workers the law was written to protect. Throughout August, Greenberg, Georgiou, and I worked seven days a week, ten hours a day, preparing for a hurricane of litigation expected to come ashore when the new legislation went into effect on August 28, 1975.

On August 28, the anticipated torrent of litigation began. Our daily working hours rose to sixteen. Soon, we learned that the Western Growers Association, and its newfound ally, the Teamsters, had joined forces in the Sacramento Superior Court. Together they sued to prevent the Agricultural Labor Relations Board from holding an election at any ranch where the grower and Teamsters had already entered into contracts. The court refused to consider the farm workers' claim that the Teamsters and the companies had entered into sweetheart contracts against the workers' wishes. Without holding a hearing, the local judge issued an order preventing the Agricultural Labor Relations Board from conducting elections. During the next seventy-two hours, Greenberg and I drafted a petition for a writ of mandate to file in the Supreme Court.

Sipping lukewarm instant coffee at 7 A.M. on Sunday morning, I sat before a typewriter silently thinking. I had been alone in the office since Greenberg had left around midnight. Lost in thought, grasping for words to explain why the Supreme Court justices should step into the farm workers' battle, I didn't hear the office door open. My heart momentarily stopped beating when I heard behind me a deep voice with a strong Southern accent. "Looks like we're all by ourselves, Jourdane."

I stared into a full white face on the shoulders of a heavyset frame. *Is this redneck here to blow me away because I messed with his way of farming? I'm too tired to fight or run*, I thought.

Nervously, I reached for the red and white Marlboro box beside the typewriter. *Who is he? Who is he?* My thoughts raced, fear circled my chest like a boa.

The massive frame approached. Suddenly, a muscular arm sprung out and grasped my shoulder. Just as suddenly, I saw a broad smile spread across the approaching face.

"I'm Bill Camp. I met you last month when I was here interviewing for a job. What're y'all doin' here in the middle of the night?"

I chuckled. "You scared the shit out of me. Yeah, I remember you, Bill. I'm working on a case. What're you doing here?"

"You might not believe this, brother, but I'm here to study Spanish."

Camp explained that he had told the general counsel when he interviewed him for the job that he could speak some Spanish. He had had a Spanish class in high school in Alabama. He thought he could speak it pretty well, but when he started working on Friday and had to talk with farm workers, he realized he was going to have trouble if he didn't learn real fast.

"So this morning," he told me, "I sneaked out of the house, trying not to wake my wife and little boy, and came down here to the office to study."

With skepticism I watched the southerner turn on a cassette player in the adjoining office and begin repeating phrases in the language he had to know to work with the Agricultural Labor Relations Board. Several hours later, a ray of sunlight shone through the office window. I got up, rubbed my eyes, stretched, and walked over to the six-foot-plus southerner.

"I'm surprised to see you working for the Agricultural Labor Relations Board," I said as I sat on the edge of a desk.

Camp smiled. "You aren't alone. I'm learning that most people in this town think all white folk with a Southern accent are members of the Ku Klux Klan. But before you and I were born, my daddy was fightin' for workers' rights. When it comes to workers, there ain't a lot of difference between the northern Alabama hills and this flat valley. Workers are workers. They're at the bottom of the ladder."

"So you're here to help change that?"

Camp nodded. "Everything I hear about this Chávez guy I like. It might take you folks a while to get used to workin' with a southerner, Jourdane, but seeing you here at seven in the morning on a Sunday convinces me we're gonna be friends. You got to believe in workers' rights, too, or you wouldn't be here."

I went back to my typewriter, glad the Agricultural Labor Relations Board had hired the big white guy from Alabama.

On Monday morning when Greenberg and I walked into the Supreme Court in San Francisco to file our petition, the clerk behind the counter told us we had a message to call the general counsel before filing anything. I found a pay phone down the hall.

"Hi, Jourdane. I know you and Greenberg worked your tails off this weekend," said the general counsel, "but I called to tell you not to file the petition."

"What?"

"Um, I spoke with the Western Growers and the Teamsters. We've agreed not to hold elections until the Sacramento trial court has a chance to decide whether we have the power."

"But we have the power. What are we here for if not to hold elections? If we back down from the start, we're admitting we're weak and will turn and run whenever someone opposes us."

"I hope you're wrong. In any case, don't file the papers. I want to have an order from the local court before we proceed."

"I'm disappointed, but you're the boss. I'll do what you say."

When farm workers across the state learned the Farm Board general counsel had given in to grower and Teamster pressure, thousands surrounded the Farm Labor Board offices with signs, "General Counsel Makes Deals" and "Farm Labor Board Sells Out."

A week later, Greenberg and I were back in the Superior Court in Sacramento. We leaned forward nervously at counsel's table, watching the elderly judge with thinning white hair straighten his slight frame.

Thirty-three

SITTING NERVOUSLY IN THE SACRAMENTO COURTHOUSE, Greenberg and I heard the elderly judge say he had thoroughly considered the papers filed by all the parties. He had read the cases each party had cited in support of its position. He was denying the growers' request for an injunction.

We walked to our car parked several blocks from the courthouse.

"It was nice to see a judge stand up to the powerful Teamsters and the agribusiness industry," Greenberg remarked.

"Yeah," I responded, "but the union says that all summer long, workers have talked about having the right to join the union. If you've ever been out in a San Joaquin Valley field in August, you've seen the workers in long-sleeved shirts, long pants, and head coverings, trying to keep the burning sun from their skin."

"I get hot hiking in my T-shirt and cut-off Levi's," Greenberg said. "I don't know how people work in the burning sun all covered."

I chuckled, but my expression became serious. "The union says that during the two weeks we waited to hear a court say it's okay to let farm workers vote in elections, growers across the state fired hundreds of union supporters, who, instead of lying in the shade during breaks, spent the summer moving from worker to worker talking about the union and the upcoming election."

That evening, I heard on television the president of the grape federation announce that on the following day they would file suit against the Agricultural Labor Relations Board. The grape federation was going to stop the Board from concealing in its secret-police manner the names of workers requesting an election.

"Shit," I mumbled when I heard the grape growers' spokesman.

144

Secret elections are going to end before they begin, I thought, *if a company can find out which employees signed cards requesting an election to let the workers vote on whether they want a union. Voting in a secret booth on a sealed and unsigned ballot won't mean anything when the company knows which workers wanted the election.*

Two days later, I drove south on Highway 99 from Sacramento to Bakersfield. My brother Tom drove east from Santa Cruz to meet me. Aware of Kern County's violent history, he decided I needed protection. In a Bakersfield motel that evening, I sat at a Formica table preparing my argument for the next morning. Tom lay on the floor nibbling remnants of our Kentucky Fried Chicken dinner while watching the World Series on television.

The next morning, I opposed the grape growers' effort to learn the names of workers who wanted an election. Meanwhile, Byron Georgiou was driving south on Highway 99 from Sacramento to Fresno to make his first court appearance as an attorney representing a client. Passing through Lodi, Stockton, Merced, and Madera, he planned the most convincing arguments he could make to a judge with the federal court for the Eastern District of California that the Agricultural Labor Relations Board policy, allowing union organizers to enter company property and speak with farm workers during the lunch break, did not deprive growers of their property without due process of law. The growers had been attacking Governor Brown's appointees to the Board because the Board had promulgated the election rule.

Georgiou, nervous when he arrived in Fresno, found his way to the federal courthouse and walked into the modern building. A clerk told him Judge Crocker was in his chambers and directed Georgiou down the brightly lit corridor. Georgiou knocked on the closed door, was told to come in, and saw the elderly jurist sitting behind an expansive desk. Sitting across from Judge Crocker was a neatly groomed lawyer. Georgiou was shocked when Crocker handed him a temporary restraining order he had already signed. Georgiou looked at the order and saw that, without holding a hearing, the judge had prohibited the Agricultural Labor Relations Board from enforcing its rule allowing union organizers to enter fields and talk with workers during non-working hours.

"We don't get a hearing?" Georgiou asked.

"Your Honor," responded the elegantly groomed gray-haired agribusiness attorney, employed by one of the nation's leading anti-union law firms who had flown in from Chicago to oppose the twenty-seven-year-old Greek novice. The management lawyer went on to say no hearing was necessary to stop the Board from engaging in Hitler tactics, and to plead for protection of his poor Japanese client from the Brown Shirts taking his property by forcing this little grower to allow union goons to trespass into his fields, crushing baby plants beneath their black boots. Before Georgiou could say a word, the non-stop attorney told the court that only it could stop the union Mafia from coercing innocent workers into joining their mob and stealing their hard-earned wages as dues to line the pockets of 'that Mussolini,' Chávez.

That evening, Georgiou told me it was too late by the time he arrived to tell the court that the Agricultural Labor Relations Board came to life through the efforts of both the agribusiness industry and the unions. The new law, bitterly contested but eventually agreed to by both the industry and the unions, was intended to reduce the violence and turmoil the San Joaquin Valley had witnessed in its fields for years. The heart of the law was free elections. The agribusiness industry had all day and each evening to try to convince its workers to vote against unionization. The Board adopted a simple rule requiring the companies to allow union representatives to speak with workers at lunch.

Ron Greenberg received similar treatment when he arrived in Tulare County that day to defend the same access rule. Greenberg said he explained to the court why union organizers couldn't talk with the workers in the evening, but the judge cut him off when Greenberg tried to argue what the National Labor Relations Board cases said. The judge brusquely reminded Greenberg that the Agricultural Labor Relations Act covered farm workers and the national law did not cover farm workers.

Greenberg reported that after he told the court Labor Code section 1148 said the courts must apply National Labor Relations Board (NLRB) precedent in enforcing the Agricultural Labor Relations Act, the judge went into his chambers, found a labor code book, read section 1148, and returned to the bench to say that section 1148 stated to use applicable NLRB precedent. But because the NLRB had no cases dealing with farm workers, there was no applicable precedent.

Greenberg asked if he understood the court to say that the phrase "applicable NLRB precedent" was meaningless because the federal law does not cover farm workers.

The court responded that if it meant nothing, it meant nothing.

That weekend, Ellen Lake—a former attorney with the Sierra Club who now worked for Board member Joe Grodin—Georgiou, Greenberg, and I spent forty-eight hours preparing another writ for the Supreme Court. Georgiou described vividly the inability of union representatives to speak with farm workers locked in labor camps. He told the court that farm workers lived in company housing and were shuttled in company buses to company fields and a large NO VISITORS ALLOWED sign was affixed to the camp gates so union supporters could not visit them in the evening. The companies kept workers in the fields during lunch and breaks, as rare as they were. Georgiou told the court about the Babcock case, in which the U.S. Supreme Court ruled that under the National Labor Relations Act union representatives may enter private company towns to speak with employees who are not otherwise accessible. Knowing this would be the first farm labor law case considered by the Supreme Court, and knowing I was a better storyteller than a legal writer, I focused on the fifteen-year farm labor struggle culminating in a law intended to provide farm workers with the rights other workers have had for forty years or more. By early Monday morning, the petition was ready. Lake and I drove from Sacramento to San Francisco and waited for the Supreme Court to open at eight.

Thirty-four

DURING THE FIRST SEVENTEEN DAYS of the Agricultural Labor Relations Board's existence, Georgiou, Greenberg, and I defended the new law in twenty-one different courts. One day we were in Monterey County, the next in Fresno. I went from courthouse to courthouse in the counties of Solano, Kern, Sacramento, Tulare, Riverside, Imperial, King, Contra Costa, San Diego, Merced, and Santa Barbara. Georgiou, Greenberg, and I fought the agribusiness corporations in state courts, federal courts, and the California Supreme Court. By early November, the eye of the hurricane had passed. The growers' petitions to block enforcement of the new law slowed to a trickle.

Meanwhile, the number of farm workers fired for supporting a union had exploded. I left Sacramento and joined an effort to stop this unlawful company conduct. I went to Salinas, where I represented a group of farm workers who said a nursery fired them after they spoke in favor of the United Farm Workers. Under California's new Farm Labor Act, as in the federal labor law, if a company fires a worker for supporting a union, the worker or the union may file an unfair labor practice charge with the Labor Board. The Board's general counsel investigates the charge. If it appears the company broke the law, the general counsel files a complaint against the company. A trial is then conducted before an impartial judge. In Salinas, I represented the workers at Kyutoku Nursery after the United Farm Workers filed an unfair labor practice charge.

The workers at Kyutoku Nursery struck on September 2, 1975, when the nursery denied their request for a wage increase. On September 3, the UFW requested on behalf of its members that they be reinstated to their jobs. The company refused. On September 4, the workers filed for an election under the Agricultural Labor Relations Act. On September 6, the Board held an election. The United Farm Workers won and was certified to represent the workers, but the nursery still would not let them return to their jobs. For a week, I was in court every day examining and cross-examining witnesses. Each evening, I interviewed witness after witness in their homes until the early morning hours. Farm worker after farm worker told me of the threats made by their supervisors.

When the week was over, the judge took the case under submission and I moved on to Santa Maria to repeat the process in a trial involving fired celery workers. Meanwhile, the hearing officer in the Kyutoku trial denied the workers relief. He found the workers' request for reinstatement to their jobs was conditioned on the employer bargaining over the wage dispute, and only an unconditional request to return to work required an employer to reinstate the worker.

When I returned to Salinas a week later, I saw Luis López. Shortly after I left Rural Legal Assistance to work for the Farm Labor Board, Luis, who had been a community worker at Rural Legal Assistance, joined me.

"How'd the nursery trial go?" Luis asked as I exited my three-year-old Toyota Corolla with 160,000 miles on it.

"Lost."

"Gonna appeal?"

"I hope so."

Luis shook his head slowly. "You know, even if you get the workers their jobs back, every worker in that company is scared. The nursery will never sign a contract with the UFW."

"I hope you're wrong," I replied. "But you probably aren't."

When Luis asked where I was going next, I told him probably the Imperial Valley.

Luis López, his sister Beatriz, and his older brother Pedro were born on a farm in eastern Mexico in the early fifties. When they were children, their father traveled to California each spring to work as a bracero, returning each fall to his family. When Pedro was ten, Luis eight, and Beatriz six, the family moved to Mexicali, hoping to immigrate to the United States. Two years later, they obtained permanent immigrant visas—commonly referred to as green cards or *micas*—and moved to the Coachella Valley.

For the next fifteen years, the López family lived in a small wooden house owned by Mr. López's employer. The children went to Coachella High School, where Pedro and Luis starred in football and wrestling, followed by Beatriz, who was very smart. Each summer the children worked in the fields for their father's employer. Rather than go out with the other workers and drink after work, the López children stayed home and read. Instead of using their earnings to buy cars, like most of their friends, they saved for college.

Pedro was the first López in the family's history to graduate from high school. During his senior year, he told his football coach he wanted to go to college after graduation. He asked if the coach would write him a letter of recommendation.

"College? You gotta be kidding," laughed the coach. "Maybe you could make it at City College, if we let them know you plan to play ball. Yeah. I'll write a letter for you to my friend over there. He can get you in, but you might have trouble. You have to maintain a C average to play ball."

"I want to go to the University of California at Riverside. Will you write them a letter?"

"They don't even have a football team."

"I don't want to play ball in college, Coach. I want to get an education."

Pedro obtained an academic scholarship to the University of California at Riverside. He was followed by Luis, who obtained a scholarship to the University of California at Santa Barbara. Beatriz, received a scholarship to attend the University of California at Riverside and later earned a master's degree at UCLA and also undertook further graduate studies at Harvard. The López family would always be proof that the American Dream can be achieved. I knew that few children of immigrants were able to send any of their children to college, but the López children accomplished the near impossible because of their parents' willingness to sacrifice.

After Luis and I talked about the nursery trial, Luis told me, "Susanna and I are gonna get married. Wanna be my best man?"

"It's about time. She's a super lady. Where and when? I'll be there," I responded, enthusiastically.

At 11:00 A.M. the following Saturday, I pulled into a parking lot behind an Indio florist shop. I walked around to the front and met Luis and Pedro.

"Is this it?" I asked.

"Yeah," Luis smiled nervously.

The López brothers and I walked toward the improvised chapel behind the flower shop. Suddenly, driving an old Volvo, Beatriz pulled up on the other side of the busy street. Susanna rushed over and told her they had to talk. The women walked into the chapel, leaving Luis, Pedro, and me on the sidewalk. A few minutes later, the minister walked up. As he entered the chapel, Beatriz and Susanna blocked his way. I overheard Susanna politely request the minister to delete the phrase "honor and obey" from the ceremony. "To honor is all right," conceded Susanna, "but obey, no. A woman is not a dog who obeys its master."

After quietly listening to a long lecture, in which the minister explained those words are a basic and established part of the marriage ceremony, Beatriz shocked the heavyset man of cloth when she said in a loud and firm voice, "Listen, minister, you either eliminate those damned sexist words or we walk, leaving you holding your sacred Bible but none of our money."

The minister conducted the ceremony as the women wished, shaking with fear under Beatriz's glare. As he read the ceremony, sweat dripped down his nose and fell onto his script. Beatriz looked over at me with a woman's-power smile. I used all my willpower to hold back laughter. That evening, I went to dinner with the López family. Beatriz and I laughed every time we looked at one another.

During dinner, Luis told me he had talked with Carlos Bowker, a field examiner for the Farm Labor Board in the Imperial Valley. "What he told me is scary," Luis said. "I wasn't going to say anything about it to you because I didn't want you to worry. But now that I've had a few beers, I feel better about telling you that you're headed into a war zone. I guess the Teamsters are dug in down in the Imperial Valley. The Teamsters have a whole lot of their sweetheart contracts down there and don't intend to give 'em up without a fight. I hope Chávez's non-violent leadership can hold out. The Imperial Valley is real close to the border. Most of the farm workers in the Valley are from Mexicali, right across the border. I think most *mexicanos* are a little too macho to turn their backs and walk away when challenged to fight."

Thirty-five

BEFORE I LEFT SACRAMENTO to work on unfair labor practice trials, the flagrant violations of the Farm Labor Relations Act caused many farm workers to believe the new law would not be enforced. Across the state, they were losing their jobs for wearing a union button or talking about having a union. The United Farm Workers demanded the governor do something. Governor Brown hired Sam Cohen, a high-powered litigator from San Jose, to come in and take control. The governor's original appointment remained the nominal general counsel, but the law would be enforced by Cohen.

I had met Cohen several years earlier when we were rafting the Tuolomne River. On many weekends during the following year, Cohen and I plummeted from boulder to boulder down California's wild rivers. Now Sam Cohen had come to save the Farm Labor Board. He had hired half a dozen hot trial lawyers and a group of highly talented Chicano investigators. Most of his crew was in the Imperial Valley, the focus of winter crop activity.

The morning after Luis and Susanna's wedding, I pulled into the parking lot behind the Labor Board's Imperial Valley office, a run-down one-story building on a bleak side street in the desert town.

The Imperial Valley is an irrigated desert in the southeast corner of the state. I was about to learn that most of its population feels far closer to Mexicali, which lies across the border, than to any city in the United States. The small town of El Centro lies in the center of the valley.

As I walked into the office, I was struck by glares from brown faces I did not recognize. I felt like a U.S. Marine walking into Baghdad while B52s bombed the country from fifty thousand feet. I asked for Sam Cohen.

"*No está*," answered the chunky receptionist.

Before I could ask when Cohen might be back, I heard a strongly accented male voice behind me, "*Eh, ése.* What you doing in the *valle?*"

I turned and recognized the speaker as Carlos Bowker, whom I had met briefly about five years earlier during a case.

"Carlos Bowker?"

"*Aquí estoy.* I heard you were coming to help us out. A lot of shit's been coming down here. The UFW and the Teamsters are preparing for war. The growers act like the law doesn't exist. The cops do whatever the growers say. You guys in *Sacra* (Sacramento) sure screwed up by selling out to the Teamsters and growers. Let's go get a *cafecito* and talk."

Suddenly, an attractive Latina in her mid-20s came through the door from a back room. Holding out her hand, she walked up to me. "You must be Jourdane. We heard a white guy was coming from Sacramento to take over our office and help us poor Mexicans out. You must be the white guy. I'm Shirley Treviño."

I took the outstretched hand and smiled. "Glad to meet you."

"As long as you know who is in charge in this office, we'll get along fine. Let me get my purse and I'll go with you guys."

Minutes later Shirley, Carlos, and I got into Bowker's old Comet sedan in the parking lot next to the office. As we rode down the deserted El Centro street, Shirley told me that Sam Cohen hired her. "We heard a white guy was coming to take charge," she said, "but we didn't think they were going to take away our power so quick."

I nodded, smiling. Shirley stared at me, smiling while I told her and Carlos about Beatriz and Susanna confronting the minister. When I finished, she said firmly, "You don't like seeing a Chicana stand up to male dominance, Jourdane?"

"I think it's good, but he is a minister," I replied.

"They had to do it. Even if the *tonto* is a minister."

I remained quiet, admiring her feminism and waist-length black hair.

In the restaurant, Shirley told me she had graduated a couple years earlier from the University of Santa Clara. While she talked, her smiling eyes appeared to be judging my naive tan face. "After graduation, I decided to stay in San Jose, so I went to work as a paralegal for Legal Aid."

I asked what she did at Legal Aid.

"Mostly I just interpreted for the lawyers. So when Sam Cohen called and said he was looking for some people to go to the Imperial Valley as field examiners for the new Farm Labor Board, I jumped at the chance."

Shirley asked Carlos how he and I knew each other.

Carlos smiled. "I've known this *vato* since you were in grade school.[1] I'm glad to see him here, even though he did sell the farm workers out in *Sacra*."

Apparently seeing my look of dismay, Carlos laughed. "No, I'm just kidding. He's done a lot for farm workers. This *vato* got the Supreme Court to hold that union organizers must be allowed to talk with farm workers in the fields during lunch and in labor camps in the evening. He got rid of the short-handled hoe. He's not one of those white liberals who come into the fields for a day or a week, talking to the press or TV about how they're saving the farm workers and then going back to their high-class suburban homes."

Hearing Carlos, I felt pride in what I had been doing for the past seven years. I asked, "Bowker, I know we know each other. But I can't remember from where. Where are you from?"

"*Aquí, ése. Del valle*," responded the light-complected twenty-two-year-old, telling me he was from there in the Valley.

"No, before."

"Such cross-examination," six-foot-two-inch Carlos grinned. "I was born in a *pueblecito* in the mountains not far from Guadalajara. I moved to the United States when I was a teenager, after selling news-

---

[1]The term *vato* is Spanish slang for "guy."

papers on Tijuana corners from the time I was five. I know you from the mental retard case, Jourdane. My high school put me in a class for the mentally retarded until they had to take me out because of your lawsuit."

Shirley stared at Carlos in amazement. "I didn't know you were in an MR class, Carlos. And this *gabacho* got you out? No wonder you think he's okay."

Carlos winked at Shirley and continued. "I'm just kidding about being in a class for the mentally retarded. After high school, I went to San Diego State University. I returned to the Valley because my family was here and there are only a handful of Chicano college graduates in the *valle*. I think I met this *vato* when he was here doing the *cortito* case."

Soon after I arrived in the Valley, I was working eighteen hours a day. I began talking almost daily with the county sheriff, whose deputies were repeatedly responding to reported conflicts between Teamsters and United Farm Workers members. Most evenings, I joined Carlos and Shirley at the office until midnight printing leaflets to advise farm workers of the rights guaranteed by the new farm labor law. Each morning at 4 A.M., the three of us were at the border passing out the leaflets to thousands of farm workers crossing from Mexicali to board company buses to carry them to California's fields. Many mornings by seven, we were in an Imperial Valley field conducting an election to enable the farm workers to decide secretly whether they wanted the Teamsters, the United Farm Workers, or no union.

Thirty-six

ON MY FIRST DAY IN THE IMPERIAL VALLEY in the fall of 1975, Sam Cohen handed me a manila folder. "This is the file on Bruce Church," he informed me, adding a few words to provide context and direction: "The trial starts next Monday. After Chávez supporters were fired, the Teamsters had filed a petition for an election. The company let the Teamsters enter the fields to speak with workers but kept the United Farm Workers out. The Teamsters won the election. It's up to you to get the workers rehired with back pay and get the election thrown out. No one has prepared the witnesses for trial yet. Good luck."

"Thanks for giving me so much time," I responded, sarcastically as I began looking through the two-inch-thick file.

On Sunday afternoon, the day before the Bruce Church trial was to start, I was at the United Farm Workers hall in Calexico, across the street from the border. I was discussing the previous election and the alleged unfair labor practices with Fred Ross, Jr., who had been the UFW's chief organizer at Bruce Church. A quiet middle-aged Mexican man came in and asked to see the state lawyer handling the Bruce Church case. The receptionist found me in the back office. I asked her to send the stranger back.

"*Buenos días, Señor abogado*. I am Jesús Ramírez," said the neat but casually dressed stranger in perfect Spanish. "Until this morning I was a supervisor at Bruce Church. I understand you are handling the case against the company."

I was surprised that part of a company's management would track me down and come into the union office the day before the trial. "Yeah, I am, and I'm kinda busy right now getting ready for the trial," I responded cautiously, assuming Ramírez was there as a company spy. "What can I do for ya?"

"For nine years I was employed as the general supervisor over all the field crews at Bruce Church, Inc. I saw the company fire many Chavistas. We had computer lists of those we suspected of supporting Chávez. We got rid of them. But the company was careful. We would wait until the Chavista made a mistake on the job or missed work or was late and fired him, so we would always have a reason."

I sat silently.

"Have you seen the wrap machines some lettuce companies are using now?" the stranger asked.

"I think so. But I'm not really familiar with 'em."

"As you probably know, in the past crews of about thirty workers cut lettuce. Each crew is divided into trios, groups of three. Two cut and one places the lettuce heads into a carton. On the wrap machines, part of the crew cuts the lettuce and part stands on a platform behind a conveyer belt that a tractor pulls through the field."

"I lost you," I admitted.

The Bruce Church supervisor explained that a lettuce machine is a conveyer belt about six feet off the ground with a platform for standing behind the belt. The belt and platform are part of a machine that moves through the field. Running back from the conveyer belt and standing platform, like a tail, is another conveyor belt that carries lettuce from the ground up to the conveyer belt on the machine. Lettuce cutters cut heads of lettuce and place them on the conveyor belt near the ground. That belt carries them up to the other conveyor belt that carries the lettuce toward the sides of the machine. As a head moves toward the side, a worker standing on the platform wraps it in plastic. It then falls into a carton that is lowered to the ground when full and is stapled shut. When Bruce Church suspected workers in a crew supported Chávez, the company put them on a wrap machine and moved the conveyor belts very fast. This forced the cutters to cut faster than normal and those on the platform to wrap faster than normal. Ramírez said it would surprise me how many workers quit when they were put on the pressure-cooker wrap machine.

As Ramírez talked, my thoughts drifted back to Hawaii when I was a seventeen-year-old surfer. I arrived in the islands with money saved from the previous summer but not enough to make it through the winter. One evening, I checked my bank account and had less than ninety dollars. The next day, I started working at Love's Bakery in Kaimuki. My job was to place brown 'n serve rolls that came by on an assembly line into a cardboard container. The container then went through a machine that wrapped it with cellophane.

When the bakery that was really a factory hired me, my supervisor showed me how to grab twelve rolls off the conveyer belt and place them in a box. "If you start to get behind, press this button to stop the line. The important part of the job is to get twelve rolls in a box before it enters the wrapping machine."

The night I entered the Love's Bakery factory on Kapahulu, not far from the backside of Diamond Head, I learned about the down side of *uku pau*. The deafening screech of machines and conveyer belts almost caused me to back out. I hadn't worked on the line four hours before facing loss of the job. The workers got two dollars an hour for eight hours or sixteen dollars a night to wrap the day's bread and rolls. This was where *uku pau* came in.

The concept is explained in George Hu'en Sanford Kanahele's 1986 masterpiece, *Ka Kanaka*. Explaining Hawaiian time, Kanahele tells about Hawaii's garbage men, most of whom are ethnic Hawaiian. In a practice that seems to have started on the sugar cane plantations, the garbage men are paid a set amount to do the job. How long it takes is up to the workers. At Love's Bakery, the experienced Hawaiians and Samoans ran the assembly line fast so they could finish the job in six hours and go home early. I loved the idea of going home after six hours and getting paid for eight, but the line moved too fast. When I began working, I stopped the machine when necessary to place twelve rolls in a box before it went through the wrapping machine. After the jeers of experienced workers turned to threats, I no longer pressed the stop button. This meant placing as many rolls into the box as I could grab before it went through the wrapping machine, six, nine, ten, whatever. I just pushed off the belt the rolls that never made it to the wrapping machine. By the time the lunch break finally arrived, I stood behind the conveyer belt across from a four-foot-high pyramid of brown 'n serve rolls.

Lost in thought in the UFW Calexico office, I chuckled. Startled when I heard, "*Señor* Jourdane?" I stared silently at the stranger sitting across the table. *Boy, did I fuck up*, I thought. *Is this all happening or am I still dreaming?*

As if Ramírez had read my thoughts, the Bruce Church field boss told me, "There's another supervisor and some foremen. We want to help you. Do you have time to meet with us?"

"Say when and where and I'll be there," I responded with skeptical enthusiasm, still doubtful, not fully believing what I had just heard.

That afternoon, seven of us met. The following day, I called Ramírez as the state's first witness. When the hearing recessed for lunch, the company's trial attorney wanted to talk about settling the case. For the next two days, I met with the corporation's labor attorney who had flown in from Orange County, and Marshall Ganz who had become the best union organizer in the country while overseeing and directly taking part in organizing for César and the United Farm Workers. In the end, one worker returned to work with a check for the pay he had lost as a result of the company's illegal firing and the company agreed to a new election enabling union organizers to enter the field to talk with workers.

As we walked to our cars from the final negotiating session, Marshall Ganz commented, "That was a pretty smart move calling that supervisor as your first witness. It really caught them off-guard."

"I think I learned the importance of surprise from my grandfather," I explained to Ganz.

One summer when we were kids, my brothers John, Tom, and I went camping in Yosemite with our grandparents. From our Upper River campsite, every day we fished and every night we watched the fireflies. Normally John and I slept outside, but one night we were in the tent because it had started to rain. In the middle of the night, our grandma awoke us, silently pointing at a large brown bear inside the tent. Inches from the sniffing bear's nose lay our three-year-old brother, Tom. John and I lay still, terrified in the darkness. Suddenly, our silver-haired grandpa moved toward the bear without making a sound. POW! He punched it in the nose. The three-hundred-pound bear looked at him, turned, and lumbered out of the tent. With one punch, grandpa became our hero forever. Later, he explained how he had learned to deal with bears as a child in Kentucky: "The most important thing is to surprise it and never show fear." From that night on, I understood the importance of surprise when facing danger and I always tried not to show the fear I often felt. I guess what I learned had paid off this week.

"Of course," I admitted to Ganz, "it helped a little when an honest man, Jesús Ramírez, walked into the union's Calexico office the day before the trial and said he wanted to talk." I smiled broadly.

Thirty-seven

In JANUARY 1976, the Agricultural Labor Relations Board held an election for all Bruce Church, Inc. employees across the state. Most Bruce Church workers moved back and forth from the Salinas Valley to the Imperial Valley to harvest the lettuce. Because harvesting occurs in the Imperial Valley in the winter, most voters were in the Imperial Valley for the election. For those who had not migrated to the Imperial Valley, an election site was also opened in Salinas. The election results were 462 votes for the United Farm Workers, 311 for the Teamsters, 17 no union, and 110 challenged ballots. Bruce Church Inc. objected to the results, claiming the election was not fair because the UFW violated an agreement on access that Marshall Ganz and I had entered with the corporation as part of the settlement several months earlier. It also claimed that the UFW had electioneered in the voting area and that the ALRB board agents were biased toward the UFW.

At the time of the election at Bruce Church, Inc., the corporation used around ten ground crews and ten machine crews when harvesting lettuce. There were between twenty-five and thirty-three workers per crew. Between 2:30 and 4:00 A.M. each morning, company buses in the Imperial Valley, including those of Bruce Church, Inc., picked up workers at El Hoyo, near the Mexicali border crossing. Driven by a foreman, each bus carried a crew to fields spread across the Imperial Valley.

The settlement agreement entered in the earlier case included authorization for one Teamster and one United Farm Workers organizer to be in the field during the day, and one organizer could board company buses during lunch to speak with workers and hand out literature. Organizers were not to be on company buses in the morning.

In its objections to the election, Bruce Church, Inc. claimed the election should be thrown out because in several instances UFW organizers went onto buses before work, and on several occasions more than one UFW organizer entered the field in violation of the agreement. The evidence showed that on one occasion an organizer was discussing a family problem with a worker when the alleged access violation occurred. On another, an organizer went to a crew in the field mistakenly believing there was not another organizer there, and the errant organizer left when he saw the second organizer.

Before the election, Bruce Church, Inc. and the unions agreed to a voting procedure that involved transporting workers to a polling site on company buses with a Board agent on each bus, and that prohibited electioneering area around the voting booths. Nearly a mile from the booths was a bridge over which buses traveled when they approached the voting area full of workers. Throughout the day of the election, both UFW and Teamsters supporters were at the bridge yelling campaign slogans.

Bruce Church, Inc. sought to show that the Board agents were biased through evidence that at El Hoyo Shirley Treviño had handed out leaflets explaining the rights guaranteed by the Agricultural Labor Relations Act. The leaflets were the ones Shirley, Carlos, and I had printed late at night at the ALRB office and passed out throughout the winter. They explained the rights that the Agricultural Labor Relations Act guaranteed farm workers. They were totally neutral, not favoring any union or any company. Bruce Church, Inc. also complained that Carlos Bowker and I had spoken at a UFW meeting before the election. Bowker agreed we had, testifying that it was the meeting to ratify a contract at Interharvest, Inc., and that we had explained to workers their rights under the Agricultural Labor Relations Act, and that we left before the ratification vote.

There was disputed evidence that for a few minutes an unknown man urged voters to vote for the UFW near the election site, and disputed evidence that another unknown man told a board agent not to forget to tell the workers how to vote. There was evidence that UFW literature was on the floor of a state car. The Board agent who drove the car, Celia Trujillo, testified that she was investigating challenged

ballots in an election involving the D'Arrigo Company and the literature was not UFW literature but leaflets she had prepared to invite the
workers to a meeting to discuss the charges in the D'Arrigo complaint. There was disputed evidence that Shirley Treviño told a crew
waiting to be driven to the polling site that the company did not want
them to vote. The parties agreed there was a delay in the bus schedule
worked out before the election and that the crew Treviño spoke with
had been waiting to be taken to the polls. Just before this incident,
Fred Ross, Jr., who was in charge of the election for the United Farm
Workers, had been told that a group of workers on machine 1, known
as *Las Tigresas,*[1] a strongly pro-Teamster crew, had roughed up members of machine crew 4, a pro-UFW crew. Members of crew number
1 had been rushing the field, confronting members of crew number 4.
The workers from crew 4 got on the bus for safety. When they were
scheduled to be taken to vote, Treviño went to tell the company supervisor that crew 4 was ready. The Board found that after unsuccessfully talking with a supervisor, Treviño told the workers that Board
agents would take them to vote in the state van because the "company does not want you to vote now."

In 1948, the National Labor Board said, "An election can serve its
true purpose only if the surrounding conditions enable employees to
register a free and untrammeled choice for or against a bargaining representative." However, in 1969 the Board said, "elections must be
appraised realistically and practically, and should never be judged
against the theoretically ideal, but nevertheless artificial standards."

Applying the principles set forth by the National Labor Relations
Board, the Agricultural Labor Relations Board was "convinced that
the incidents complained of, including those relating to Board agent
conduct, were not sufficiently substantial in nature to create an atmosphere which renders improbable a free choice of voters." In making
this determination, the ALRB found that both Teamsters and UFW
organizers were entering the fields to speak with the workers in tech-
nical violation of the agreement, but the company restricted the UFW

---

[1] *Las Tigresas* is a Spanish language variant of "the female tigers."

organizers and not the favored Teamster organizers. The Board pointed out that during the weeks before the election, the company general manager, Michael Payne, put on an aggressive leaflet campaign favoring the Teamsters over the UFW. The Board concluded that the election results were not affected by noisy demonstrations at the voting site, Treviño saying she thought the company was delaying movement of the buses, leaflets that may have appeared to be union literature on the floor of a Board agent's car, or any formal mismanagement of the election. On December 13, 1977, the ALRB accordingly certified the UFW as the bargaining representative of all farm workers at Bruce Church, Inc.

In June 1978, the United Farm Workers and Bruce Church, Inc. entered into a six-month contract based in large part on the previous Teamster-Bruce Church contract. During the six-month period, the *Tigresas*, apparently angry that the Teamsters had lost the earlier election, had, in the words of the hearing officer who heard testimony at a later unfair labor practice hearing, engaged in a "nasty encounter" with UFW leader Dolores Huerta and caused a wildcat strike.

After the contract terminated on December 31, 1978, the company and union began negotiating the terms of a renewed contract. While most of the lettuce companies negotiated as a group, Bruce Church, Inc. decided to negotiate alone with the union. For two years, the United Farm Workers and Bruce Church negotiated. The union was asking the lettuce companies to pay the workers $5.12 an hour, an amount the growers felt was outrageous. In February 1979, the Bruce Church workers struck in an effort to nonviolently put pressure on the company. They tried to return to work the following month, but Bruce Church, Inc. refused to allow them to work, claiming they had been permanently replaced. When an economic striker is permanently replaced, the striker has no right to regain his or her old job until a vacancy occurs. When a worker is striking because the company has committed an unfair labor practice, however, the aggrieved employee has a right to return to work if he or she chooses to do so, regardless of whether the company has permanently replaced him or her. When a union is certified as the bargaining representative for a company's employees, the union and the company have a duty to bargain in good faith. If the company is not bargaining in good faith, it is committing an unfair labor practice and must rehire striking workers whether they have been permanently replaced or not.

During the summer of 1979, protesting the growers' refusal to enter contracts with the UFW, ten thousand farm workers and other supporters marched to Salinas's Hartnell College from San Francisco, one hundred miles to the north; San Ardo, seventy miles to the south; San Juan Bautista; and Watsonville. Joining Chávez were Governor Jerry Brown and actress Jane Fonda. At the rally, Chávez announced the signing of a contract with Salinas Valley's Meyer Tomato Company. Union attorney Jerry Cohen noted that the contract "makes a lie of the industry claim they could not afford our demands." In the fall, lettuce harvesting moved to the Imperial Valley. On December 27, 1983, the Agricultural Labor Relations Board held that Bruce Church, Inc., had not been negotiating in good faith.

Because of the extreme poverty in Mexico and Central America, caused in large part by the United States' world economic dominance, hundreds of thousands of undocumented men and women had begun, each year by this time, to cross the U.S. border seeking jobs. Agribusiness corporations in the United States were thus increasingly able to pit these impoverished immigrants against the low-paid members of the United Farm Workers. When UFW members wanted to strike for more tolerable working conditions, in this context, their chances of success were diminished by the growers' ready access to hungry Mexican and Central American immigrants. Facing this dilemma and committed to nonviolence, César Chávez sought to urge Bruce Church, Inc. to enter a contract with its workers through a boycott of Red Coach Lettuce.

Twenty years earlier, the grape boycott had broken the will of Delano growers, thus leading to a number of contracts. Chávez wanted to replicate this success to force Bruce Church to honor the UFW's collective bargaining status and rights in California lettuce fields. To end the dispute with Bruce Church, Inc., Chávez thus asked shoppers to stay away from markets that sold Red Coach Lettuce. Under prevailing state laws, Chávez's call for a boycott of Bruce Church was legal in California but not in neighboring Arizona. Although the union was careful to limit use of the boycott in states where it did not violate the law, in apparently seeking a friendly forum, Bruce Church, Inc. filed suit against the union in Arizona claiming the California boycott had spilled over into Arizona in violation of that state's law. After a thirty-one-day trial, a jury held against the union and ordered it to pay Bruce Church, Inc. a little over $5,400,000. The union appealed and the Arizona Supreme Court reversed the award, finding that the trial court had erred in allowing the jury to find the union must pay damages for its actions outside of Arizona. The Court sent the case back to trial to see if the union had caused any damage through acts performed in Arizona.

While the case was being retried, César Chávez underwent two days of grueling cross-examination by Bruce Church attorneys. During the night of April 22, 1993, after the second day of examination, the nonviolent struggler to improve the treatment of farm workers died. Bruce Church, Inc. obtained an order for the union to pay $2,900,000. The attorney representing the union in a second appeal, San Diego's Michael Aguirre, said the amount would bankrupt the union. He maintained, "César Chávez was facing an unfair set of pressures on him . . . that's what killed him."

Six days after César's death, fifty thousand farm workers and supporters accompanied his body as it was carried from a central Delano park to Forty Acres, the union headquarters several miles west of town. Bishop Roger Mahoney of Los Angeles said mass and performed final rites over César's casket. With a short-handled hoe resting atop the wooden box Richard Chávez had made to bury his brother, César was lowered into the ground.

In May 1996, under new leadership, Bruce Church, Inc. ended a seventeen-year struggle and entered into a contract with the United Farm Workers. Arturo Rodríguez, the new union president, hoped to build a "partnership of cooperation."

Meanwhile, few other companies where the United Farm Workers is certified to represent the workers have entered a contract. In the summer of 2002, believing the companies were refusing to bargain in good faith, Dolores Huerta, at the side of Arturo Rodríguez, marched with farm workers across the San Joaquin Valley to Sacramento to urge Governor Gray Davis to sign a law that would end the stalemate.

In an editorial, the Salinas *Californian* urged Governor Davis to sign the bill, saying, "It's the right thing to do." The Salinas daily went on to explain that growers who bargained in good faith had nothing to fear. If Governor Davis signed the new law, the editorial reasoned, they would "continue to resolve problems in the way they had done it for nearly 30 years—under the auspices of the state's landmark Agricultural Labor Relations law." Governor Davis did sign the law. Now, if a company refuses to bargain in good faith with the union chosen by its workers in a free and fair election, a neutral party or arbitrator appointed by the state will step in and settle the conflict.

The growers have vowed to challenge the law in the courts.

The Salinas Valley has grown in population and agribusiness greatly, but in other ways has changed little since John Steinbeck lived there and told us what's East of Eden. Driving through the Salinas Valley today, there are more houses and there are portable toilets attached to company buses parked on access roads strewn across the fields, where there were none thirty-five years ago. And there is drinking water for the workers. The workers stand tall holding long-handled hoes instead of stooped to the ground raising and lowering a *cortito*. But farm laborers are still the lowest paid workers in the United States, while suffering to perform the nation's hardest work. There are tens of thousands of farm workers who voted in secret elections seeking a contract between their employers and their union, the UFW. The Agricultural Labor Relations Board has certified the United Farm Workers as the bargaining representative for these tens of thousands of workers, and the law requires their employers to bargain in good faith with their union, but still there are few contracts.

Jerry Cohen and his incredible staff of idealistic young lawyers have moved on. Marshall Ganz is teaching organizing at Harvard. Eliseo Medina, César's longtime aide, is running the Service Employees Industrial Union (SEIU) for the Western United States. Salinas

Strawberries is gone, Pic n Pac is gone, Bruce Church is gone, and Interharvest is gone, but there remains the same dark-brown earth John Steinbeck saw seventy years ago and the same dark-brown farm workers César Chávez and Dolores Huerta worked to organize. There is also the continuing good work of CRLA.

In May 2002, the *Monterey Herald* reported that growers were fighting a bill that would prohibit them from forcing workers to stoop over and remove weeds by hand. Mexican-American children are no longer labeled retarded, but if their English is not good enough they are still segregated into dead-end tracks. Bleak labor camps still scar the countryside like acne. Undocumented workers are treated worse than ever. Since the September 11, 2001 terror attack by foreigners, it is more difficult for hundreds of thousands of honest but hungry immigrants to enter the United States, and hundreds if not thousands have died trying to cross the southwestern deserts. Meanwhile, farm workers' earnings continue to drop as inflation rises, growers continue to refuse to enter into contracts with the United Farm Workers, and the federal government continues to add restriction after restriction to the legal services clients can receive and the kind of cases public interest attorneys for the poor can bring. With the restrictions comes less money to provide legal assistance to the growing clientele. But the United Farm Workers under the tenacious guidance of Arturo Rodríguez and California Rural Legal Assistance under the astute leadership of José Padilla continue the fight, living the words of César Chávez and Dolores Huerta, *Sí Se Puede*. The landscape has changed a little, but the struggle continues.

Additional titles in our
Hispanic Civil Rights Series

Message to Aztlán
Rodolfo "Corky" Gonzales
ISBN 1-55885-331-6

A Gringo Manual on How to Handle Mexicans
José Angel Gutiérrez
ISBN 1-55885-326-X

**Eyewitness: A Filmmaker's Memoir of the Chicano
    Movement**
Jesús Salvador Treviño
ISBN 1-55885-349-9

Pioneros puertorriqueños en Nueva York, 1917–1947
Joaquín Colón
ISBN 1-55885-335-9

The American GI Forum: In Pursuit of the Dream, 1948–1983
Henry A. J. Ramos
Clothbound, ISBN 1-55885-261-1
Trade Paperback, ISBN 1-55885-262-X

**Chicano! The History of the Mexican American Civil Rights
    Movement**
F. Arturo Rosales
ISBN 1-55885-201-8

**Testimonio: A Documentary
History of the Mexican-American Struggle for Civil Rights**
F. Arturo Rosales
ISBN 1-55885-299-9

171

They Called Me "King Tiger": My Struggle for the Land and Our Rights
Reies López Tijerina
ISBN 1-55885-302-2

Julian Nava: My Mexican-American Journey
Julian Nava
Clothbound, ISBN 1-55885-364-2
Trade Paperback, ISBN 1-55885-351-0

César Chávez: A Struggle for Justice / César Chávez: La lucha por la justicia
Richard Griswold del Castillo
ISBN 1-55885-364-2

Memoir of a Visionary: Antonia Pantoja
Antonia Pantoja
2002, 384 pages, Clothbound
ISBN 1-55885-365-0, $26.95

Black Cuban, Black American
Evelio Grillo
2000, 134 pages, Trade Paperback
ISBN 1-55885-293-X, $13.95

Hector P. García: In Relentless Pursuit of Justice
Ignacio M. García
2002, 256 pages, Clothbound
ISBN 1-55885-387-1, $26.95

The Life and Times of Willie Velásquez
Su voto es su voz
Juan A. Sepúlveda, Jr.
2003, 384 Pages, Clothbound
ISBN 1-55885-419-3, $27.95

La Causa
Civil Rights, Social Justice and the Struggle for Equality in the Midwest
Gilberto Cárdenas, Editor
Foreword by A. J. Ramos
2004, 224 Pages, Clothbound
ISBN 1-55885-425-8, $28.95